# CASH DIET

PERSONAL FINANCE DEMYSTIFIED

## CHRISTOPHER SAVOY

HONORÉ PRESS

Cash Diet

Personal Finance Demystified

By Christopher Savoy R.T.(R)(T)(CT) MSRS

1. BUS050000 2.BUS050010 3. BUS050030

Print ISBN: 978-1-7343401-0-5

Paperback ISBN: 978-1-7343401-1-2

Ebook ISBN: 978-1-7343401-2-9

Library of Congress Control Number: 202098062

Printed in the United States of America

Honore' Press, LLC

16337 Keystone Blvd.

Prairieville, LA 70769

cashbudgetcajun.com

❀ Created with Vellum

# CONTENTS

# POSTER CHILD

There were three posters that adorned the rooms of nearly every boy growing up in the 1980s. Number one was the *Top Gun* movie poster. Every kid I knew decided, at least for the summer of 1986, that they were going to be a hot shot fighter pilot when they grew up. The second most popular poster among boys of the 80s was anything with a picture of a Lamborghini Countach on it. Whether it was featured in front of an Italian villa, or being lathered up for a wash by a bikini-clad babe, the Countach was our ultimate pin-up dream car.

The third most popular poster, a picture of a garage, became an icon of 80's excess that had us all pushing to increase our ACT scores. In the foreground, a four-car garage dug into the side of a hill. In the distance, a Spanish-style California McMansion overlooked the ocean. Smack in the middle, a helicopter was landing in the front yard. Just off to the right of the helipad was a large yacht backed by a yellow-orange 80's sunset complete with the silhouette of a palm tree. The focus of the poster, the garage, was occupied by the following symbols of 80's machismo: the obligatory Countach, a Porsche 911, a 500 series Mercedes sedan, and a BMW 325i convertible. The caption at the top of the poster read *"Justification for Higher Education."* That poster, probably intended as a tongue-in-cheek shot at inspiring young minds, ultimately summed up the decade of excess that was the 1980s.

That poster, and many other aspects of 80's culture, reinforced the idea that college existed as a path to material gain—that earning a degree basically guaranteed you the success touted by such symbols. It's no wonder my generation graduated college with such an over-riding sense of entitlement. I believed that any college degree was "good enough" and it really didn't matter which major I chose. I thought that money was the most important factor in happiness and that my college degree would provide it in ample supply. I believed having a cool car would make me somebody and that a McMansion was in my bright, not-to-distant future. Nothing could have been further from the truth.

Five years after college graduation, I had little money, no tangible future, a pile of debt, and a divorce. Worst of all was the fact that I was the last person on earth I thought would end up this way. After all, I was raised by a loving family, had no vices, studied hard, and was never in trouble at school or in the community. People like me were supposed to just graduate and succeed, as if the process of growing up were automatic. My generation (now called Generation X) was more or less told, "If you go to college, you will be successful and great things will happen to you."

### Cash Diet

By age 28, I was the poster child for the typical Gen Xer. I was unsatisfied with my career path, deep in debt, and haunted by a lack of purpose. After months of research and personal reflection, I made the toughest decision of my life: I returned to college to pursue a degree in radiologic technology. My biggest fear at the time was the cost of the schooling. Not wanting to add to my debts, I lost sleep over whether or not my new income would be enough to overcome the additional student-loan payments. To accomplish this new goal and make my new career worth the cost of the education, I would have to do things differently—*radically*. I would have to put myself on a Cash Diet. I went on to earn that degree, and two more, one-hundred percent debt-free! With my new income and near-limitless opportunities for extra work, I paid off my old debts, invested in retirement, and started budgeting money the way my family had taught me two decades before. My wife and I have gone on to achieve financial stability and true personal wealth, and it is my mission to help you do the same!

What exactly is a Cash Diet? Simply put, the Cash Diet is a financial lifestyle choice. The Cash Diet rejects loan debt, credit cards, "interest free" financing, and automotive debt in favor of paying up front. Utilizing the values of simplicity, contentment, and discipline, the Cash Diet commits you to putting in a few years of hard work up front in order to reap the benefits of debt freedom later on... and what bountiful benefits they are! Imagine what life would be like if you had $1000, $1500, or even $2000 cash left over after paying bills every month. You could fund a dignified retirement, pay cash for vacations, and have hobbies. Debt promises to provide us with all of these things but, instead, traps us in a prison of our own design.

### Break the Chains!

There is a new undercurrent in American culture. A new financial counterrevolution that is fighting against the debt-creep and misinformation that has plagued us for at least three generations. The housing crisis that started in 2008, followed by a lackluster economy and unprecedented student debt, is prompting Millennials and Generation Z to question the place of debt in our society. Like the Silent Generation who retracted their trust in banks after the Great Depression, our country's young people are learning to take financial literacy into their own hands. Yet, our consumer-driven society continues to extol the virtues of debt. In the face of a system and a society determined to keep us in financial chains, how do we even begin to resist?

Luckily, sound personal finance boils down to just a few key decisions. Get them right, and you will look forward to a lifetime of happiness followed by a dignified, even wealthy, retirement. Get them wrong, and a lifetime of struggle ensues. A debt-free college education is a great way to start on the right foot. Choosing the right career —the first time—will prevent you from having to deal with the expense of returning to school later in life. Purchasing used cars for cash rather than financing new cars at full price is a sure way to give yourself the gift of financial freedom. Purchasing your first home the right way, under the right circumstances, will prevent you from falling victim to calamities such as the housing crisis of 2008. Communicating with your partner and living below your means (on a budget) will keep your goals on track. Having a cash account for emergency situations will defend you against unexpected events like the current crisis created by Covid-19. These decisions can make or break you financially, so it pays to get them right—the first time.

Equal part memoir, nostalgia trip, and instruction manual, *Cash Diet* aims to guide readers through the pitfalls and possibilities of personal finance in today's complex, consumer-centric society. This is a simple, common-sense guide to handling money the way people did long before Americans financed everything from vacations to bicycles. If you are a Gen Xer or Millennial looking to get out of debt, or a member of Generation Z who wants to stay out of debt in the first place, this book is for you! If you're looking for a sophisticated manual on how to win big in the stock market or make money flipping homes, this book is *not* it. If you dread a book filled cover to cover with complex equations, fear not. If my description of this journey sounds like it may appeal to you, then continue on; I have a feeling you will enjoy reading this book as much as I've enjoyed writing it.

# 1

## IT CAME FROM THE 80S

There were only two things you needed to know to successfully navigate childhood in the Savoy home. Number one: Dad is always right. Number two: Save your money. While growing up in the Savoy home, saving money was as natural as breathing. It was an intricate part of our family culture. Every Sunday, my sister and I were paid a small allowance for completing the prior week's chores. Mom saw that some of our allowance was stored safely in the local bank, and dad encouraged us to give a portion to the church. Our allowance was small; I believe it was five dollars or so a week starting at five years of age. The amount of money was reflective of our age and responsibilities. Over the years, our weekly allowance grew along with those responsibilities. Sometime around six years of age, I began to accompany mom to the bank. I remember going to the teller to hand off my crumpled bills for safe-keeping. Back home, I had another bank in the form of a plastic Donald Duck that received regular deposits right into a slot on top of his blue beret. Our parents started us early on the road to sound money management. We were saving, tithing, and spending. It's no surprise that these three actions are key components to personal finance recommended by virtually every money-management guru. And yet, my sister and I were beginning these habits before we learned to read. To this day, I believe that first handful of wrinkled ones and fives (now converted to pixels) is still sitting at the bottom of my bank account making up the foundation of all my savings and net worth.


## The South Stadium Engineers Society

My father was the first person in our family to attend college. As the son of a housewife and welder, my father spent much of his time helping on the family (his grandparent's) farm while excelling in school. His mother was very intelligent in her own right and had been the first in our family to graduate high school. Her education served her well after she lost my grandfather at the young age of 42 and had to support herself by working for a local general store. I have no doubt that my grandmother recognized dad's talent for math and science and pushed him to excel. My father graduated valedictorian of St. Amant High School in May of 1966. Though many high-paying jobs were available to him at that time, the promise of an even brighter future (not to mention the draft) moved him to postpone instant gratification for a degree in mechanical engineering at Louisiana State University. The road to a college degree would be fraught with challenge.

In the 1960s, scholarship funds didn't flow as freely as they do today. Additionally, (and perhaps, thankfully) federal student loans were not the force they are today. My dad would have to earn an entire year's tuition, room, and board each summer between school years: and earn he did. While many young people were partying away their college summers, my father spent the bulk of his time sweating in the 120-degree hell of empty boiler tanks. He toiled for hours grinding, cleaning, and inspecting the tanks for cracks. The work was hot, miserable, and extremely dangerous. A summer at the plant typically netted about $300. In the mid to late 60s, that was enough money to cover tuition, books, and room and board for two semesters at LSU.

Dad was disciplined in his studies and active on campus. He and a few classmates formed a loose fraternity called the South Stadium Engineers Society. Dad excelled, as always, and became our family's first college graduate in December 1970. Within a few months, my father was employed as a mechanical engineer at the Texaco refinery in Convent, Louisiana—just a few miles from our family's homestead. It was during this time that he placed the next block on our family's foundation.

Upon starting his career, dad took an immediate interest in stocks, mutual funds, and retirement savings. Pension plans and Social Security were still the popular retirement plans in those days, but dad had a natural distrust of both. He saved additional monies utilizing stocks and mutual funds in hopes they would help to bolster his retirement in case of pension problems or some lack of availability of Social Security funds. After my sister and I came along, he began putting away money for our college education as well. All this sounds very familiar by today's standards, but in the 1970s, few people were looking this far ahead. This was evidenced by the fact that, out of a class of 400, I was the only person I knew that had a college savings. Maybe it was dad's natural curiosity that led him to research financial planning. Perhaps the untimely death of his father instilled in him the importance of leaving us an education nest egg. Whatever the reason, dad made the unselfish sacrifice of putting our future ahead of his wants.

### A Place Called College

Although I didn't realize it at the time, I was growing up during America's greatest economic boom since the 1950s. Everyone was making money. The toys, clothes, music, movies, and popular culture of the 80s have since reached mythological status. In spite of the noise, distraction, and temptation, my father's rock-solid discipline ensured that we were living below our means. If the neighbors financed a new car every five years, dad paid cash for one every ten years. When the style was Levi's 501s, dad sported Rustler jeans from Walmart. Mom and dad lived on a budget, and my sister and I were made keenly aware of it. It wasn't always easy, but we understood that our parents were making sacrifices for us so we could go to a place called "college."

College certainly worked out well for my father. Dad's engineering degree offered great rewards upon graduation. During dad's college years, the United States was racing to beat Russia to the moon, and American industry was growing as a result. Even though my family lived a relatively frugal existence compared to our peers, the effect of the 80's economy was still palpable. My sister and I had all the toys and went on epic vacations. We had everything we needed and most of what we wanted. In the 1980s, we simply didn't know how well we had it. My sister and I had never known a time when America struggled. We had heard the stories from our parents and grandparents, but we thought that tough times were long ago, far behind, and never to return. The latter part of the 1990s were about to give us context about how great it really was to be a child of the 80s. With the dot-com bubble preparing to burst, the yet-unanticipated terrorist attacks of 9-11, and the impending crash of the housing market on the horizon, my first decade after college was about to show me how tough life could be. It's not that these events caused me to drift through a decade of career stagnation, but they certainly didn't help. The truth is, I made key errors in my decision-making that made it difficult for me to compete in the workplace. The first was my college major.

# ALLOW ME TO INTRODUCE MYSELF... TO MYSELF

In the mid 90s, LSU was working hard to maintain its status as one of America's great party schools. Louisiana had the nation's loosest liquor laws, and nowhere did the beer flow freer than smack in the middle of the LSU campus. Every Thursday night, the courtyard of West Laville Hall featured live music, dancing, and two kegs. A fifteen dollar "recreation fee" and date of birth before September 1st 1976 ensured participation in the festivities. Unlike the many productive extracurricular activities available to me, I never missed a Thursday social.

There was a particular girl I remember well. We had met at one of those Thursday socials, and I took an immediate liking to her. Just as I was beginning to believe the friendship was headed somewhere, she quite bluntly stated her opinion as to why she could not see me seriously. She said, "You don't know who you are Chris." She expressed those few words with such conviction that you would have thought the words "I DON'T KNOW MYSELF" were tattooed on my forehead! To a woman's sensibilities, perhaps they were. At the time, of course, this was the silliest and most pretentious thing I had ever heard.

The young lady was absolutely correct in her assessment. She had sensed through our conversations that I was passively floating through life. She understood that I was running from my fears instead of running toward any substantive goal or aspiration. To this day, I believe other women saw this as well but did not speak up to me about it. Instead, they just kept their distance. At the time, I saw myself as a devout Catholic, though I wasn't regularly attending mass. I touted a future in the design arts but participated in nothing other than design class. I described myself as a hard worker, yet I did not have a job. I contradicted myself and was too blinded by my own feelings of entitlement to realize the truth. I didn't know or understand myself at all. That fact might as well have been tattooed on my forehead, after all.

## 2

---

# REDUCE YOUR COLLEGE DEBT

When I started LSU in the fall of 1994, I had no idea who I was or what I was supposed to do. I knew I liked working with my hands, but I felt that skilled labor was looked down upon. I deeply respected my dad's accomplishments as an engineer, but I knew I wasn't fit for a cubicle at the plant. I settled on interior design. As a student, I would be building models and drafting; both were enticing hand skills. I felt that I was artistic and needed to explore that side of myself. Interior design offered me the opportunity to do that. My downfall? I picked a major I was interested in studying rather than a career I was passionate about. Deep down inside, I had an unsettling feeling that I wouldn't find work in the field and that maybe I was pursuing the wrong major. I brushed those thoughts away, convincing myself that college graduates of any type were in demand and that my life would be better if I earned a degree. I had given in to some dangerous myths about what a college degree can offer.

*"A college degree is my ticket to success."*

If a college degree isn't absolutely required for your career field of interest, college can't do anything for you. In the 80s, popular culture placed college on such a pedestal that my generation piled into the dorms in droves; many of us clueless as to who we were or what we wanted to do. Most people I know (myself included) have never used their bachelor's degrees.

### *"I need to go to college to find myself."*

You don't need to pay $100,000 to find yourself! You need to know who you are *before* you enroll in college! Going to college to find yourself is like buying a Walmart because you need socks. There are many cheaper ways to find your calling. Hike the Appalachian Trail. Enroll in the Peace Corps. Join the armed forces; they are experts at stripping away the bull and putting you directly in touch with who you really are in just a matter of months. They'll even pay your tuition! If you need to take a year or so off, do it! Just don't rely on some college classes to help you figure it out.

### *"You have to start college right after high school."*

Gen Xers and Millennials were fed the idea that they needed to go straight to college the day after high school was over. We were told things like, "If you don't go now, you never will." I realize that starting college right away has always been a tradition; but first, we should look at the circumstances surrounding the time when those traditions were set in place. From the 1940s until the mid 70s, a student could earn all they needed for one year at a state college by working a summer job. My dad earned enough during the summer to pay for tuition, room and board, books, and supplies for one year at LSU! While it's still possible to do this with the right job, it's still a difficult task. The idea of going straight to college became cemented in place during the Vietnam War, when 18-year-olds could avoid the draft by enrolling in college. I think my father's generation just couldn't let go, as most of my friends and I were pushed hard to go straight to college... and not lose a minute's time. A year seems like an eternity to an 18-year-old. However, by age thirty, having taken a year off to figure things out will be totally insignificant!

### *"A degree in general studies will allow me to work in a variety of industries."*

A degree in general studies means that you don't have enough education in any particular skill to be of use to anyone. A general studies degree is a direct ticket to a cubicle in a credit card customer service call center. Remember that giant warehouse at the end of *Raiders of the Lost Ark*? You are the Ark, the crate is your cubicle, and you will be filed away among the endless stacks of boxes never to see the light of day again. Figure out what you want to do before settling for a general studies degree so you don't end up like that crate at the end of *Raiders*.

### *"Community college is not as good as the state school."*

A community college is the best value in post-secondary education that you will find. Period. You can expect to be able to cash flow your first two years of school at community college—something that would be much more difficult at an "elite" university. The smaller class sizes also make for a more intimate experience, with true contact between the faculty and students. As for the argument that state universities offer a "better" education; nearly all state schools accept community college credits; meaning, those state schools have placed their endorsement on community colleges. You can almost view your local community college as an extension of your state university system. Community college is as good, if not better, than an elite state school. At the very least, it will save you considerable money.

## Ways to Reduce Your College Costs

There is nothing that will kill your spirit faster than having to spend the first ten years of your career handing out a huge chunk of your paycheck back to Sallie Mae. You're supposed to go to college in order to learn how to prosper, not how to linger. In spite of what you have been conditioned to believe, crushing student debt is not necessary, it's not normal, and it hasn't always been around. My father paid his way through school. When I returned to college, I earned three degrees without using debt. The path to a debt-free education is not easy, but it exists, and it starts with the following tips.

## Scholarships: A Full-Time Occupation

The internet offers almost limitless scholarship opportunities. I am willing to bet that you could apply online for scholarships 24 hours a day your entire senior year and still only scratch the surface of what is available. Of course, it does help to focus your efforts. Just about every college major has some sort of student association. Those associations often offer scholarships. You need not limit yourself to the student associations either. I'm sure there are many trade associations related to your chosen career. They too offer scholarships to current and prospective students; such was the case when I was working on my master's degree. I received two large scholarships through my national trade association that nearly paid for the entire program. Don't forget the organizations that your parents and other family members are involved in. Wherever and however you choose to hunt down scholarship money, it should be your full-time occupation your senior year of high school!

## Attend Community College

Tuition at my local community college is currently 66% less expensive than at my nearest state university. That amount of money makes the difference between being able to cashflow an education versus having to take out loans. Spending two years at a community college will add up to thousands of dollars in tuition, fees, and interest saved!

## Your State School Is Good Enough

Colleges love to advertise all of the top-notch research they're doing. The commercials are exciting, too. Students in lab coats are busily mixing chemicals and firing lasers while solving world hunger and ending homelessness. I'm not saying these things don't go on at the average college campus. Just keep in mind that the life of an average student will look absolutely nothing like the exciting experiences displayed on television during halftime. Whether or not your college experience is as exciting as the commercial is entirely up to you because your college experience is what you make of it. Consider that before venturing off to pay out-of-state tuition because you feel that another school is better or more exciting. Your state school is good enough!

## Live at Home If Possible

If you live within one hour of a community college or university, there is no need to live on campus. Living in a dorm at LSU was a luxury that my dad afforded to me by saving up for 18 years. If I had to do it over, I'd live at home and bank the dorm fees. I realize that gas is a factor, but you'd have to live really far away to spend more on gas than rent. Which brings me to my next argument.

### Don't Take Out Cost of Living Loans!

One of my biggest beefs with student loans is that lenders will allow students to take out loans for non-study-related expenses. I consider room and board a non-study-related expense. I have peers that owe more in student loans taken out for living expenses than for tuition! Before you sign up for massive loan debt, think about this: The money you borrow today to live in a stuffy dorm or cheap apartment is money you *won't* have tomorrow to buy the home of your dreams! College should help you achieve your dreams, not force you to postpone them!

### Never Give Up on Scholarships!

A common mistake among college students is that they give up applying for scholarships after high school graduation. In my experience, scholarships are easier to obtain with some college experience. There are plenty of scholarships and grants available to students who are already in college! Maybe your ACT scores weren't stellar. I never scored higher than a 22 on the ACT, yet I made the dean's list at LSU my first semester. I was able to get support for three degrees later in life because I could show the grant administrators that I was an academic achiever in spite of my standardized test scores. If you work hard in college, you may be able to convince an organization or two that you're worth their support!

### Get the Most Value out of Your Degree

You've managed to cut your college costs by working part time and earning scholarships and grants. You have made the wise decision to live at home while attending two years of community college before moving on to your nearest state school. You offset remaining costs by working a job that pays better than fast food or retail. You've done a great job of getting the most out of your money. So, how do you make sure you're getting the best value for your money? As with most things in life, you get out of college what you put into it. The following suggestions will help you get the most out of your college experience.

### Understand What You Stand to Gain

*Accounting Principles* magazine polled 507 graduates in 2018. The results were disheartening. Only 17% of those polled had enough funds to cover the basic items listed on the survey. This included rent, food, phone, car payments, and student-loan debt. Barely one-fifth of the survey participants were able to pay for necessities and afford to spend on entertainment and hobbies.[1] Nearly all of those polled agreed on one thing: They would have made different choices given the chance. One-third stated they would have sought more scholarships or financial aid. Another third expressed that they would have sought a higher-paying career track. The remaining third of the participants indicated they would have worked and saved more during college. Although I completed my bachelor's degree twenty years ago, I share many of the sentiments expressed in this survey.

### Understand What Life Actually Costs

After college graduation, the real world taught me some tough lessons about what it actually costs to maintain a household and what you need to earn in order to do more than just scratch out a living. My choice of major would have been better served by a more thorough evaluation of careers and salaries. The truth is, I did very little research. Not wanting to repeat past mistakes, I painstakingly researched every financial aspect of my second career choice. From starting pay to shift differentials and PRN (part-time) work, I had a firm grasp of what life would look like as an X-ray tech. I even went to the trouble of calculating my taxes, Social Security, health insurance, and retirement deductions. When I graduated X-ray school, there were no surprises. My take-home pay was within 5% of what I had predicted it would be two years earlier.

## Think Twice About Nobility

Banish the idea that money doesn't matter as long as you enjoy your work. Sure, money might not matter when you are single and childless, but that condition can change quickly. What you should be asking yourself is, "Will this career generate enough income to raise a family and still allow for a comfortable retirement and for some fun along the way?" My first career involved recruiting boys into a youth program. For $27,000 per year, I got to spend lots of time camping and hiking. It seemed like a ton of money... until I began looking ahead. I asked myself, "How far will this money stretch when I have a wife and children?" Think about this: As of 2018, the poverty line for a family of four in the United States is $25,100. Imagine yourself supporting a wife and two children on $30,000 per year. Consider that before going to school for that low-paying career you feel so passionate about. After all, nothing corrodes passion faster than struggling to make ends meet. Yet, thousands of young people sign up for crushing student debt every day in exchange for the privilege of starving in a "noble" profession.

## Network or Not-work

During my time at LSU, I placed too much stock in the fact that I was earning a degree and paid too little attention to networking. My hope was to challenge the notion that it's less about *what* you know and more about *who* you know. I focused on being an expert while neglecting to network in the design community. The old adage turned out to be true (much to my disadvantage). After returning to college later in life, I stumbled upon some memorable advice. While walking the halls at X-ray school, I overheard a lecture in a nearby class. The instructor was encouraging his students to get involved and to network. He said, "Network, or not-work." I was not only eavesdropping on some very practical advice, I was being inadvertently reminded of the shortcomings of my past. Since that day, I've held on to the idea of "network or not-work" and re-doubled my efforts to stay connected with my profession through community and professional activism.

## Get Involved

In my dad's day, jobs were plentiful and college graduates were in relatively short supply. As a result, there was far less competition for jobs than there is today. Many of my peers (myself included) took for granted the idea that a college degree was some sort of ticket to success. I believe that many of us felt a deep sense of entitlement to all the things we grew up with and figured our degree would just make our success appear. I shunned the idea of involvement, much to my own demise. Today, a higher percentage of high school graduates are heading to college and creating a more competitive job market. Anyone expecting to find work within a few months of graduation must already have connections in the marketplace.

To get the most out of your degree, do the opposite of what I did during interior design school and get involved! Every college program has some sort of student's association on campus that articulates with local trade associations. For example, the ASID (American Society of Interior Designers) met monthly and worked closely with designers in our community. I might have made valuable connections with those individuals, except for one major problem: I never attended the meetings. It doesn't matter if you are a nursing, architecture, engineering, or accounting student; chances are you have the opportunity to meet professionals in your area through your student association. I recommend that you become active today and even consider holding office in your association. Upon graduation, you will have a stellar resume and strong references. You might have an offer or two from professionals you met through involvement with your association. Remember, *"network or not-work."*

# THE BUCKET LIST

December, 2013. It's winter in Natchitoches, Louisiana, and Michele and I are enjoying the Christmas lights strung along the Caddo River. The lights, an annual tradition made famous in the movie *Steel Magnolias*, had been on our bucket list of things to see for several years. We'd arrived just a few hours earlier for another bucket-list item: a graduation ceremony. That morning, I had become the first person in my family to earn a master's degree. My grandmother was the first person in our family to graduate high school. My father, in turn, was the first to earn a college degree. Continuing education has always been a theme in my life; therefore, I was determined to carry on our family's tradition of education as far as was practical for my career.

As I shook the dean's hand and looked across the crowd, I thought, "I've done what so many say is impossible." I had earned three degrees in nine years without using student loans!

After my divorce in 2004, I returned to college to pursue a degree in radiologic technology. I was convinced that it was not worth pursuing if I had to spend another ten years slogging through student debt. I applied for countless grants and scholarships for individuals re-educating into the medical field. I was awarded a grant through the Workforce Investment Act. It covered tuition, books, uniforms; even gas and car repairs! I completed the program in May 2007, then worked weekend night shifts making $22.00/hr. Because I only worked on the weekends, I spent the following year earning a post-graduate certificate in radiation therapy. I completed the radiation therapy certificate in one year and started working in that field for $25.00/hr.

After paying off some old debt and getting my hands on a paid-for beater, I made plans to cash flow my master's degree. However, I encountered a problem. I had saved up plenty of cash after paying off my debts. I was making sacrifices to build up my savings, and I didn't want to let the money go so easily. After shopping around, I found a very reasonably priced ($10,000), high-quality program at North-western State University in Natchitoches, Louisiana. I decided to apply for more grants and scholarships to help offset the tuition. Over my two-year master's program, I received $6,500 in scholarship funds! I earned my master's degree having spent only $3,500 out of pocket!

# 3

## THE CAREER STAIRSTEP

The naysayers will have you believe that a debt-free education is impossible. I know they're wrong because I accomplished it myself. The truth is that colleges use unclear pricing and unfair tactics to force students into making snap decisions. The banks, already woven into the college websites, swoop in "to the rescue" with unlimited funds to "help" students "achieve their dreams." Don't get pulled into it. Go into college armed with a common-sense plan—and follow it.

One of the best features of the medical field is that just about anyone can easily stairstep their way from janitorial staff all the way up to the surgical suite and beyond, if they so desired. Allow me to explain. Hospitals employ a vast number of individuals whose backgrounds span the entire spectrum from housekeeping to CEO and all points in between. Hospitals also hire a wide range of professionals. Doctors, lawyers, accountants, HR specialists, nurses, allied health professionals, educators, compliance personnel, physicists, and more can all be found within the walls of one facility. What does that mean for a college student? For one, there are so many entry-level jobs in hospitals. What's more important is that many of these jobs must be filled 24 hours per day. Hospitals are rich with good-paying jobs that operate during all hours, creating a flexibly-scheduled revenue stream for college students. Additionally, hospitals typically pay what is called a *shift differential*—a boost in hourly pay to work on evenings, nights, and weekends. A resourceful, hard-working student could easily parlay these opportunities into a system that puts them through college debt-free!

### The Career Stairstep
### *Step 1: The Part-Time Job*

Imagine a series of jobs that will work like a debt snowball for your career. Each job will pay significantly more than the one before. This will allow you to pursue your next level of education utilizing the pay increase you receive at each step. I call this a career-stairstep plan. The general idea is the same as the debt snowball. In the debt-snow-ball plan, you pay off a debt and then roll the money you are paying each month into the next largest debt. You never take a raise when you pay a debt; rather, you continue living the same lifestyle while banging away at your debt. The career stairstep is similar in that you do not increase your lifestyle until you are through. Each time you meet an educational goal, you move to a higher-paying position. You then utilize your increased pay to cash-flow the next level of education you wish to pursue. The medical field is ripe with opportunities to apply such a plan.

Let's say you dream of becoming an RN. You have committed yourself to not taking on student debt, but you have no college nest egg. Start out with a part-time job at a hospital (full-time if you are already out of high school). The job can be anything. Housekeeping, cafeteria, patient transportation, etc. What is most important is that you choose a job where you have access to odd hours and weekends in order to work around your school schedule. Take advantage of the higher shift differential whenever and wherever possible. (As noted earlier, shift differential is extra pay for working odd hours and weekends.) Focus on work and save everything you can. Save like crazy and push on 'till you wear holes in your socks! You won't be needing a fancy wardrobe... you'll be working in scrubs. Work hard, save hard, and sacrifice hard. Within only a few months, you should have enough money saved to advance to the next step.

### Step 2: The Certificate Program

You have probably heard radio ads from one of the many schools offering certificates for EKG, phlebotomy, or medical assistant. I like these three programs in particular because they're generally afford-able and can be completed in a short time. With hard work and focus, a dedicated student can save enough money to pay cash for one of these programs and complete it within a reasonable time frame. A high school student could probably earn enough cash working part-time from age 16-18 to take one of these classes right after high school graduation. Again, what's really important here is that these jobs pay higher than your typical minimum wage retail job and may offer access to shift differential.

According to Indeed.com, the average pay for a phlebotomist in the United States is around $12.50/hour.[1] Try earning that much folding clothes at the mall! A typical phlebotomy/EKG/lab certificate will take two semesters. A high school graduate with some money saved could attend the summer and fall right after graduation and be ready to earn $26,000 the following year.[2] That number could increase with overtime, PRN, and shift differential. "But Chris," you may be asking, "What about the students who take a traditional path, won't they be so much farther ahead?" They will be ahead in classes, but only by one semester. You must also consider the crushing debt those students will collect after only one year of school. Meanwhile, you will be earning enough money to self-fund the next step in your journey.

### *Step 3: Your Chosen Field*

Fast-forward through your sophomore year of college. You've been working as a phlebotomist on the evening shift while attending your nursing pre-requisites during the day. It's been a tough road, but you've been generating about $33,000 per year between your hourly rate, shift differential, and occasional overtime. You've picked up lots of holidays as well. The last two years have been the hardest of your life, but you are ready to apply for the nursing program—and you are 100% debt-free! Best of all, your experience as a phlebotomist has made you very familiar with the hospital where you will be a nursing student. You have been around for compliance checks and CPR classes. You've already completed the mandatory online learning so common in hospitals these days. You are experienced with starting IVs and drawing labs; so much so that you will become invaluable in assisting other students in your program. You have also absorbed everything you've seen and heard the last two years. You won't even realize your own depth of knowledge until you begin your nursing classes in a few weeks. And all of your anxiety about being accepted into the RN program? It turns out that your hospital experience and work ethic made you a shoe-in candidate for acceptance!

The next two years will bring many new challenges. Nursing school requires more intensive study and your class schedule will not be as flexible. As a result, you may have to cut back on work hours. It's ok, though. You saw that coming and planned ahead. You have already saved some money to help subsidize your income. At this point, you might be one semester behind your peers. Don't panic! When you graduate, you will have earned true freedom by not having to pay student debt!

### *Step 4: Beyond Undergrad*

Using this plan, I was able to stairstep myself through graduate school using zero debt. You might recall that I earned a grant for X-ray school which allowed me to attend debt-free. When I decided it was time to return to school for my graduate degree, I had the money already set aside. Only, something very interesting happened. I found myself attached to the money I saved and decided I didn't want to let it go. As a result, I began hunting for scholarships to cover my graduate degree costs. I was able to earn two scholarships that nearly covered the $10,000 tuition cost. I'm so glad I didn't just cave in and take out a loan like so many others. I'm glad I attempted to seek out grant money before paying out my own.

The trouble with student debt is that once you take out the first loan, it tends to snowball with every consecutive level of education you pursue. You finish your bachelor's degree, but the ten-year $300/mo. payment makes it difficult for you to self-fund your graduate degree. Then what do you do? You take out another loan, thus adding to your misery and extending it further. This process continues until you're staring at a $700/month student-loan payment. Worse yet, your graduate degree was only good for about $450/month in extra income. At that point, you have to question whether the whole thing was a mistake. I see this happen every day with young people and it breaks my heart. Break the cycle! Being debt-free will allow you to self-fund that graduate degree. If you are really resourceful, you will earn a few grants and scholarships along the way. I know because I did it myself.

## Apply the Plan to Virtually Any Career

I used a medical career stairstep as an example for two reasons. First, careers in the medical field are particularly easy to stairstep because of hospital schedules and the many opportunities available for advancement. And second, my familiarity with medical careers also allows me to cover a medical stairstep in great detail. With a little imagination and resourcefulness, a career stairstep plan can be applied to most occupational pathways.

Remember, what is important is that you start off in a job that is in some way related to your field of interest. Work odd hours and weekends to maximize your pay and save your money. Start off with community college classes instead of major universities to stretch your money farther while working and saving for the next step. If you're pursuing a degree in architecture, interior design, or landscape architecture, be on the lookout for jobs in construction. While you're at it, volunteer for organizations like Habitat for Humanity. Both will provide invaluable insight into how your designs will actually be built (and it looks great on your resume).

Landscape architecture lends itself especially well to the career stairstep. You could start your own lawn business with equipment from the pawn shop and branch out your business into landscaping while in school. As an added bonus, a lawn business will allow you flexible hours while paying better than retail or fast food. Keep your grades up, and after your first year of college, apply for scholarships again. This time, apply with organizations tied to your chosen career and those that are tied to extracurricular activities in which you have participated on campus. You might be surprised to find that there are many organizations out there that are making funds available to students who are already in college. Sometimes, these organizations are more likely to overlook not-so-perfect ACT and SAT scores if they see that you're dedicated and involved. I will repeat it again: This method worked for me and can work for you, too!

By applying the career-stairstep plan, you will be so busy that your college years will fly by. Before you know it, you'll be out there earning a living. Best of all, you won't be sending a large chunk of your hard-earned money to Navient! But beware, our culture is ripe with debt-creep and misinformation about money. Learning to budget your money will go a long way in ensuring that your money is working as hard for you as you are for it.

# STAR WARS AND THE ZEN OF DELAYED GRATIFICATION

There exists no adult in my generation whose life wasn't touched in some way by the cultural zeitgeist that was (and still is) the *Star Wars* saga. I attended all three of the original trilogy movies in our local theatre. I don't remember the first *Star Wars* movie because I was only one year old at the time, but mom assures me I was there and that I was quite a handful. *Star Wars: The Empire Strikes Back* would be the first *Star Wars* film I would remember, and it left quite an impression! There were giant robot camel-tanks, blasting laser cannons, and swashbuckling laser-swords! Even at four years old, the key parts of the film were burned into my long-term memory. Come Christmas of 1980, I would re-tell the entire movie on Santa's lap while impatient families waited for me to describe each character and vehicle toy in expressive detail. Fortunately for me, the Christmas Elves at Kenner were already fulfilling desires I didn't even know I had through their legendary line of *Star Wars* toys. 1980 and 1981 brought Christmas trees flowing with action figures and vehicles from *The Empire Strikes Back*, and I was hooked! *Star Wars* was in the toybox, on top of the bed, and in the sock drawer. Every morning, you could eat *Star Wars* the cereal, brush your teeth with *Star Wars* the toothbrush, then ready yourself for school by washing up with *Star Wars* the soap and *Star Wars* the shampoo. A pair of *Star Wars* Underoos and a Han Solo t-shirt completed the ensemble. Unfortunately, the joy of opening a new X-Wing and being greeted by the smell of fresh petrochemical bliss was limited to Christmas and birthdays. If I wanted to expand my collection, I would have to save up and buy the galaxy one piece at a time.

There was a general store in the nearby town of Gonzales. Lebeuf's carried a little bit of everything. Lebeuf's was sort of like Walmart except smaller. Walmart had not yet opened in our area to grace us with its orange Formica décor and built-in hot dog stand. Lebeuf's was well-known among my peers as having a decent selection of toys. It was no Sears or Service Merchandise, but the latest from *Star Wars*, *Transformers*, *GI Joe*, and *Go-Bots* could be snatched up there. When mom announced a trip to Lebeuf's, I would hastily pull the plug underneath my Donald Duck bank and relieve his innards of small bills and pocket change. After gathering what I could, I was off to discover what awaited on the toy aisle.

Accustomed to seeing displays full of the now-classic 3-3/4" *Star Wars* figures, I was taken aback by what appeared to be something new and different. The orange and red box displayed not a single figure or vehicle, but an entire backdrop from *Empire Strikes Back*. This new plastic wonder was a miniaturized re-creation of the iconic scene were Luke learns of his parentage after losing his hand to the burning slash of Vader's lightsaber. The toy set piece stood 4" tall and was populated with several painted metal figurines. Two of them were Luke Skywalker in different poses, and the other two were Darth Vader. In spite of their 1-1/4" stature, the figures were extremely detailed and highly expressive. Needless to say, I knew where my seven dollars would go that day.

As with all *Star Wars* toys of that period, the box art was almost as joyful as the prize that awaited inside. Colorful pictures, action layouts, and fun character bios gave the recipient plenty of eye candy to pour over. My eyes met the back of the package with excitement as

I discovered there were other sets that could attach to mine! The toy wizards at Kenner had done an excellent job grabbing my attention. I suddenly felt... incomplete. I had to collect the remaining pieces of the set to quell the rising emptiness.

Unfortunately for the good folks at Kenner, the *Star Wars Micro Collection* did not resonate with all children as well as it did with me. Parents already strapped by the purchase of 3-3/4" scale figures and their large expensive space vehicles chose not to invest in another toy line of a different scale. Many kids simply didn't like the non-posable metal figures. Whatever the case, the *Micro Collection* was dropped after only one year. I had discovered my first piece of the toy line very near the end of its production run. In fact, the stores were running out of backstock as I decided to collect the other two parts of the playset. The clock was running, and I had no idea how little time I had.

Blissfully unaware of the *Micro Collection's* fast-approaching fate, I formulated a plan to bring this shoebox-sized piece of the *Star Wars* universe into my toybox. Scrounging up a pencil and paper, I scribbled out the foundations of my first-budgeted purchase. I had three dollars left after the purchase of the first component. The remaining components were the Bespin Control Room ($7.00) and the Freeze Chamber ($25.00). Which one should I go for first? I had three dollars left from the last trip to the toy store. After tithing and bank visits, I could have the seven dollars for the Control Room in just two weeks and have one dollar left over. This would give me a "quick win." I could save enough money for the third component in ten weeks for a total completion time of three months. Of course, three months for a seven-year-old might as well have been three years. Even though three months seemed like an eternity, I resolved to pursue the goal. Besides, I would have the first two components to keep me busy in the meantime.

It wasn't long before I began sharing my quest with peers at school. Most of my friends shared in my excitement about completing the playset. There were, however, a few naysayers. One classmate in particular (the kid who had the coolest toys, snuck them to school, and never shared them with anyone) thought my plan was very silly. His recommendation was to borrow money from my parents and pay them back with my allowance after I make the purchase. That idea sounded okay. After all, this was the kid with all the cool toys. And he wasn't the only one taking advances on his allowance. There was one problem, though: The thought of borrowing money felt alien and grotesque. The idea of not having my allowance for three months while paying back my parents made me nauseated. Why did I feel this way when borrowing money came so natural to those around me? Was I born this way, or was my reaction due to the way I was being raised? Were other children's propensities to borrow natural, or were their parents teaching them to borrow by offering to loan them money?

In spite of the reactions of some classmates, I stuck to the plan. After saving money for three months, I was disappointed to discover that Lebeuf's was no longer carrying the *Star Wars Micro Collection*. Mom assured me that dad would try to call around and locate the much-sought-after Freeze Chamber. That evening, dad phoned several retailers in order to locate my prize. I sat nervously on the plush carpet of his study as he dialed store after store. Just when I felt my dreams were crushed, dad slammed down the phone and shouted, "Service Merchandise!" They claimed to have just one remaining, and dad rushed me there very near closing time. As I rode home with my prize in hand, I swelled with pride! Taking the time to save the money nearly cost me the chance to complete my goal, but I met it nonetheless. That very day, an idea took root in my mind: *Planning and patience will win the day even in the face of uncertainty.*

Mom and dad must have paid special attention to my affinity for the *Star Wars Micro Collection* toys because several more of them would pop up in stockings, at birthday parties, and under the Christmas tree. I'm guessing they picked up the toys on clearance as the line dwindled. This multiplicative effect is one that money guru Suze Orman often eludes too: *If you handle money properly, it will multiply in ways you didn't expect.* To this day, my Bespin World playset is my most cherished *Star Wars* collectible. I saved money for what seemed like an eternity. I felt the agony of waiting for each week to slowly lumber past and the ecstasy of seeing all the parts finally assembled. Best of all, my allowance was safely intact after the purchase. As a result of the time and effort I put into that acquisition, the Bespin World playset has survived countless garage sales and purchase offers. I took great care as a child not to damage the set or lose any of the pieces or figurines. The lesson? *You more deeply cherish and care for the things you save for.*

And that is how, at seven years old, I made my first budget and stuck with it in spite of the naysayers that surrounded me. I would go on to budget for every toy, piece of clothing, or car part that I wanted, ignoring the "conventional wisdom" of others telling me to borrow money.

# 4

# YOUR BUDGET: A FRAMEWORK FOR FINANCIAL SUCCESS

When discussing a framework for financial success, there is no more literal a framework than your monthly budget. Your budget is the structure, the skeleton, on which your finances are constructed. Without a budget to construct your financial plan, your money (and quite possibly your future) takes on a shapeless and ineffective form. You probably remember grade-school science class lessons about your skeletal system. Without an underlying structure of bones, you would collapse into a shapeless mass on the floor. With no bones to provide leverage, your muscles would be useless, quivering blobs unable to gain traction or move forward. Such is your finances when living without a budget.

Your monthly budget accomplishes several important tasks. It lets you know at a glance how much money you have to work with at any given time. Conversely, it also lets you know at a glance what expenses are due at any given time. A well-designed budget listed out on a spreadsheet (in a program like Excel) should tally your income and expenses and calculate your disposable income for the month.

My budget typically has two columns: a "budgeted expenses" column and a "spent" column. As you can see in Table 4.1, the budgeted expenses column displays what I believe I will pay for each line item, while the spent column displays what I actually spent on each item. Some budgeted items will be the same every month (e.g., your house payment). Others, like your power bill, may vary. For example, the first line item in my budgeted expenses column is groceries. I budget about $400 per month (your grocery needs may be more or less). Just to the right of that column is the spent column for groceries. As I purchase groceries during the month, I tally my spending in the spent column. When I've reached $400, that line item has reached its terminal point—i.e., there is no more money for groceries that month. I tally all items down each column. Some items will inevitably go over budget, but some items fall under budget. The name of the game is to follow the budget close enough that, at the end of the month, the numbers in the spent column on the right match the numbers on the budgeted column on the left. Budgeting may be a struggle for the first few months. Many Americans who are not budgeting simply don't know what they spend per month on groceries, personal items, entertainment, etc. It's important to stick to the system for several months, making adjustments where necessary. After a few months, you'll have a much better idea of what it takes to run your household and where you can make changes.

**Table 4.1: Sample Household Budget**

| Categories | Budgeted | Spent |
|---|---|---|
| <u>Home</u> | | |
| Mortgage Payment | $835 | $835 |
| | | |
| <u>Utilities</u> | | |
| Cellular | $140 | $140 |
| Power | $95 | $95 |
| Water | $75 | $75 |
| Internet | $60 | $60 |
| Natural Gas | $25 | $25 |
| | | |
| <u>Transportation</u> | | |
| Fuel | $300 | $280 |
| Repairs / Maintenance | $100 | $120 |
| Car Ins. | $160 | $160 |
| | | |
| <u>Household Expenses</u> | | |
| Groceries | $400 | $400 |
| Household | $50 | $10 |
| Personal Items | $50 | $50 |
| Clothing | $50 | $0 |
| Pets | $50 | $50 |
| | | |
| <u>Savings</u> | | |
| Cash | $1,000 | $1,090 |
| Christmas Club | $50 | $50 |
| | | |
| **Total** | **$3,440** | **$3440** |
| | | |
| <u>Income</u> | | |
| Spouse 1 | $2000 | $2000 |
| Spouse 2 | $1500 | $1500 |
| | | |
| **Total** | **3,500** | **$3500** |
| | | |
| **Remainder** | $60 | $60 |

My budget is divided into categories such as home, utilities, savings, and transportation. Under home, you will find the mortgage payment, groceries, home supplies (hardware), and personal items. Utilities include power, water, gas, internet, and cellular service. Transportation includes fuel and car insurance. There is another line item under transportation that is intended for maintenance items, such as oil changes, tire rotations, etc. The savings section (my personal favorite) includes local savings, investments, and vacation savings. In actuality, these all get deposited into the same account. What matters is that I know how much of my savings account is dedicated to each of those items. My spreadsheet is designed to calculate that, too. Sometimes, Michele and I decide to save for a special item as well. Whatever that item may be (it's currently a pair of kayaks), it has a dedicated line item in the budget under savings.

Notice at the very bottom of the example budget there is a line titled "remainder." My spreadsheet subtracts the total of all budget items from our total take-home income to calculate a remainder. The object is to design your budget so that the remainder is as close to zero as possible without going into a negative sum. This means all of your money for the month is assigned to something. Notice that the example budget shows a remainder of $60. In your case, you would assign that money to another line item, bringing the remainder to zero. That something could be some new shoes, a date night, a donation to your favorite charity, or extra money for the savings.

There are many budgeting spreadsheets available online and as part of software such as Excel. If you're computer savvy, a budget spreadsheet just like this one can be put together in under 30 minutes. If building a spreadsheet in Excel isn't your thing, try searching the #debtfreecommunity on Instagram. On accounts such as @easy_budget and @thebudgeteer, you'll find budget designs, snowball calculators, and amortization schedules that are both attractive and easy to use!

Why is it so important to track money in such a specific manner? It helps keep your priorities in check. Believe it or not, there are people out there who receive a paycheck only to run out and buy some item they want. They continue on with the month not realizing they forgot some bill was due or some non-regular expense was coming up. All of a sudden, the light bill is due and there isn't enough money to cover it. People who handle money this way often end up charging their needs on a credit card after purchasing their wants out of their paycheck.

## Money Measurement Tools

Once you have established a budget, it's important to track your overall success. A budget, while being a great tool, is merely a one-month snapshot of your financial path. Once you've mastered your monthly budget, it helps to look at some additional indicators to get a feel for the big picture. Your net-worth calculation can help you determine if you're on the right track. This might sound very sophisticated, and perhaps that's why many people misunderstand net worth. However, if you've mastered your monthly budget, your net worth will be easy to calculate. Let's clarify and discuss how your net-worth calculation can help you design your financial future.

## Net-Worth Calculation

The net-worth calculation is often misunderstood as an individual's annual income. Net worth actually has nothing to do with salary. In fact, there can be individuals with super-high salaries and little or no net worth (and even negative net worth). At the same time, there are individuals with lower salaries and high net worth. How is that possible? It all depends on what you make vs. what you spend. That is, quite simply, the essence of the net-worth calculation. The net-worth calculation looks similar to a budget. It's broken down into two main sections. The "assets" section lists all items of value, such as your cash, investments, home, and autos. The "liabilities" section lists all monies that you owe: car notes, credit cards, mortgage debt, car debt, etc. Your assets and liabilities are totaled separately, then your liabilities are subtracted from your assets. The remainder is an individual's net financial worth. Review the example shown in Table 4.2. I've left the entries blank so you can focus on how it's set up. After familiarizing yourself with the layout, continue to Table 4.3 where we will plug in some real-world numbers.

## Table 4.2: Net Worth Calculator

### Assets

| | |
|---|---|
| Home Value | $_____ |
| Vehicle 1 | $_____ |
| Vehicle 2 | $_____ |
| Cash Savings | $_____ |
| Investments | $_____ |
| Retirement Savings | $_____ |

**Total Assets**          $_____

### Liabilities

| | |
|---|---|
| Home Mortgage | $_____ |
| Vehicle 1 Loan Balance | $_____ |
| Vehicle 2 Loan Balance | $_____ |
| Credit Debt | $_____ |
| Student Loans | $_____ |

**Total Liabilities**          $_____

## Total Assets − Total Liabilities = Net Worth

As you can see, the net-worth calculator uses very simple math. Anyone with basic computer skills can build this spreadsheet in Excel, or if they prefer, with pencil and paper. Perform this calculation at least once a year, and save each one so you can watch your growth over a period of many years and decades.

. . .

Next, I would like to demonstrate a net-worth calculation sheet that is filled out by an imaginary couple. For this exercise, we will assume our couple has been married for ten years and currently earns $100,000 per year. Our couple is investing and saving but has a full complement of debt payments in their liability column.

## Table 4.3: Net Worth Calculator

### Assets

| | |
|---|---|
| Home Value | $220,000 |
| Vehicle 1 | $10,000 |
| Vehicle 2 | $15,000 |
| Cash Savings | $10,000 |
| Investments | $50,000 |
| Retirement Savings | $200,000 |
| **Total Assets** | **$505,000** |

### Liabilities

| | |
|---|---|
| Home Mortgage | $110,000 |
| Vehicle 1 Loan Balance | $12,000 |
| Vehicle 2 Loan Balance | $18,000 |
| Credit Debt | $25,000 |
| Student Loans | $50,000 |
| **Total Liabilities** | **$215,000** |

**Total Assets** ($505,000)

-

**Total Liabilities** ($215,000)

=

**Net Worth** ($290,000)

As you can see, our couple has a net worth of nearly $300,000. Let's perform that calculation again (Table 4.4). This time, we will assume our couple struggled early on to clear their debts before committing to a cash-only lifestyle. We will assume the same home value and mortgage debt. However, we will omit the credit card, auto, and student debt present in Table 4.3. The value of the automobiles in the assets column will reflect cash cars of lesser value.

## Table 4.4: Sample Net Worth Calculator

## (Without Debt)

### Assets

| | |
|---|---|
| Home Value | $220,000 |
| Vehicle 1 | $8,000 |
| Vehicle 2 | $3,000 |
| Cash Savings | $10,000 |
| Investments | $50,000 |
| Retirement Savings | $200,000 |
| **Total Assets** | $491,000 |

### Liabilities

| | |
|---|---|
| Home Mortgage | $110,000 |
| Vehicle 1 Loan Balance | $0 |
| Vehicle 2 Loan Balance | $0 |
| Credit Debt | $0 |
| Student Loans | $0 |
| **Total Liabilities** | $110,000 |

**Total Assets** ($491,000)

-

**Total Liabilities** ($110,000)

=

**Net Worth** ($381,000)

Without all of the debt payments from the first example, our couple has a whopping $381,000 net worth! Now, imagine that our couple had put down just $20,000 more on the purchase of their home. That $20,000 would now be omitted from the liability column, thus moving their net worth over the $400,000 mark. This drives home an important lesson. The nicest homes and most expensive cars speak little to the net worth of an individual. If someone is investing in depreciating assets, such as expensive automobiles, they're essentially adding to the liability column while subtracting from the asset column. A person who is living in an extravagant home but is not saving or investing is performing a similar equation. That person is shorting one set of assets (savings and investments) for another large asset (an extravagant home) that comes with a large liability (a mortgage balance). Therefore, it's possible to look like you're a high-networth individual when, in reality, you may have a negative net worth or just be breaking even.

I like to perform my net-worth calculations annually. I typically perform the calculations in January of each year shortly after receiving fourth-quarter statements from each of my investments. I estimate my home's value utilizing sales of similar homes in my neighborhood. Vehicle values are calculated with *Kelley Blue Book*. It's important to re-calculate vehicle values each year in order to account for depreciation. Yes, vehicles are assets that lose value with each passing year (all the more reason to reduce your losses by driving used cars). Your retirement and investments will, on most years, demonstrate growth due to interest and additional principle. On the liability end, your mortgage debt will decrease over time, thereby bolstering your net worth. This is true for the other debts you are paying down as well. As you pay down debts in addition to your mortgage, it is important that you do not pick up new debts to take their place. You will be surprised to see how fast your net worth accumulates once your debts are paid off for good. Michele and I have only our mortgage debt remaining. We have pledged to ourselves to no longer use credit cards or automotive debt. As a result, we have seen year-to-year increases in our net worth that has surprised even me. Speaking of year-to-year, keep your net-worth calculation each year and compare it to each subsequent year. Before long, you should see annual growth!

## Annual Growth

The annual-growth calculation is very simple and can be performed once you have two subsequent measurements of net worth. Pretend that you performed a net-worth calculation in January of 2017. Your net worth at that time was $100,000. One year later, in January of 2018, you performed a net-worth calculation with a result of $112,000. It's easy to see using these particular numbers that you experienced a gain in net worth of $12,000 or 12%. To arrive at your percentage growth, subtract your prior year's net worth from your current net worth. Divide the result by last year's net worth, then and multiply times one hundred. The equation will look like this:

$$\$112,000 - \$100,000 = \$12,000$$
then:
$$\$12,000 / \$100,000 = .12$$
then:
$$.12 \times 100 = 12\% \text{ Growth}$$

The idea is to have positive growth every year by paying off debt, increasing savings, or making money on your investments. Preferably, you will achieve all three. Personally, I am not satisfied with anything less than 10% growth per year. Fortunately, I have surpassed that goal every year since I began calculating growth.

## What Will This Cost Me (Thirty Years from Now)?

Mastery of personal finance demands that you always have an eye on the future. Whether you're budgeting for next month or planning next year's vacation, you should be looking at your needs for the next five years at the very least. You should be calculating your retirement savings progress and paying attention to what your account balance could be 30+ years from now. Perhaps you've just had a child. Hopefully, you are looking ahead 18 years and preparing for your child's education. Whatever your goal or purpose, personal finance demands that you always look ahead.

Every purchase is a choice. It's a choice between the purchase you are considering and the money you have in hand. Once your money is spent, your money has virtually disappeared. It doesn't matter if you've purchased a car, an item of clothing, or a piece of furniture. That item is worth less than what you paid for it the very moment you walk out of the store. When you make purchases, your money is gone forever. If you choose to save your money, it will continue to live on and manufacture more money (if invested properly). Some items don't present you with a choice. For example, we must all eat and have shelter to survive, so we never stop to weigh our money against the grocery bill or rent. But what about luxury purchases? Jewelry, clothing, furniture, accessories, hobbies, etc.? Those purchases present a choice between having *money* (which will bring more wealth if treated properly) or having *things* (which will strip wealth through depreciation). Every purchase affects your future. Make all of your purchases with careful thought and deliberation.

When it comes to especially large purchases, it helps to consider what an item will cost you 30 years from now. For example, let's say you're getting engaged and shopping for the right ring. And let's also say you're a great saver and you happen to have $10,000 cash. Should you spend that whole amount? Try asking yourself: What will this purchase cost me 30 years from now? If I were to invest this $10,000 in mutual funds, how much wealth will it have generated over 30 years? What will I miss out on if I fail to invest this money? This concept is known as *opportunity cost*. In other words, what growth opportunity was missed by not investing this money? We can use Table 4.5 to make that calculation.

**Table 4.5: The Future Value of an Investment**

| n | 1% | 2% | 3% | 4% | 5% | 6% | 7% | 8% | 9% | 10% |
|---|------|------|------|------|------|------|------|------|------|------|
| 1 | 1.01 | 1.02 | 1.03 | 1.04 | 1.05 | 1.06 | 1.07 | 1.08 | 1.09 | 1.1 |
| 2 | 1.02 | 1.04 | 1.061 | 1.082 | 1.102 | 1.124 | 1.145 | 1.166 | 1.188 | 1.21 |
| 3 | 1.03 | 1.061 | 1.093 | 1.125 | 1.158 | 1.191 | 1.225 | 1.26 | 1.295 | 1.331 |
| 4 | 1.041 | 1.082 | 1.126 | 1.17 | 1.216 | 1.262 | 1.311 | 1.36 | 1.412 | 1.464 |
| 5 | 1.051 | 1.104 | 1.159 | 1.217 | 1.276 | 1.338 | 1.403 | 1.469 | 1.539 | 1.611 |
| 6 | 1.062 | 1.126 | 1.194 | 1.265 | 1.34 | 1.419 | 1.501 | 1.587 | 1.677 | 1.772 |
| 7 | 1.072 | 1.149 | 1.23 | 1.316 | 1.407 | 1.504 | 1.606 | 1.714 | 1.828 | 1.949 |
| 8 | 1.083 | 1.172 | 1.267 | 1.369 | 1.477 | 1.594 | 1.718 | 1.851 | 1.993 | 2.144 |
| 9 | 1.094 | 1.195 | 1.305 | 1.423 | 1.551 | 1.689 | 1.838 | 1.999 | 2.172 | 2.358 |
| 10 | 1.105 | 1.219 | 1.344 | 1.48 | 1.629 | 1.791 | 1.967 | 2.159 | 2.367 | 2.594 |
| 11 | 1.116 | 1.243 | 1.384 | 1.539 | 1.71 | 1.898 | 2.105 | 2.332 | 2.58 | 2.853 |
| 12 | 1.127 | 1.268 | 1.426 | 1.601 | 1.796 | 2.012 | 2.252 | 2.518 | 2.813 | 3.138 |
| 13 | 1.138 | 1.294 | 1.469 | 1.665 | 1.886 | 2.133 | 2.41 | 2.72 | 3.066 | 3.452 |
| 14 | 1.149 | 1.319 | 1.513 | 1.732 | 1.98 | 2.261 | 2.579 | 2.937 | 3.342 | 3.797 |
| 15 | 1.161 | 1.346 | 1.558 | 1.801 | 2.079 | 2.397 | 2.759 | 3.172 | 3.642 | 4.177 |
| 16 | 1.173 | 1.373 | 1.605 | 1.873 | 2.183 | 2.54 | 2.952 | 3.426 | 3.97 | 4.595 |
| 17 | 1.184 | 1.4 | 1.653 | 1.948 | 2.292 | 2.693 | 3.159 | 3.7 | 4.328 | 5.054 |
| 18 | 1.196 | 1.428 | 1.702 | 2.026 | 2.407 | 2.854 | 3.38 | 3.996 | 4.717 | 5.56 |
| 19 | 1.208 | 1.457 | 1.753 | 2.107 | 2.527 | 3.026 | 3.616 | 4.316 | 5.142 | 6.116 |
| 20 | 1.22 | 1.486 | 1.806 | 2.191 | 2.653 | 3.207 | 3.87 | 4.661 | 5.604 | 6.727 |
| 21 | 1.232 | 1.516 | 1.86 | 2.279 | 2.786 | 3.399 | 4.14 | 5.034 | 6.109 | 7.4 |
| 22 | 1.245 | 1.546 | 1.96 | 2.37 | 2.925 | 3.603 | 4.43 | 5.436 | 6.658 | 8.14 |
| 23 | 1.257 | 1.577 | 1.974 | 2.465 | 3.071 | 3.82 | 4.74 | 5.871 | 7.258 | 8.954 |
| 24 | 1.27 | 1.608 | 2.033 | 2.563 | 3.225 | 4.049 | 5.072 | 6.341 | 7.911 | 9.85 |
| 25 | 1.282 | 1.641 | 2.904 | 2.666 | 3.386 | 4.292 | 5.427 | 6.848 | 8.623 | 10.834 |
| 30 | 1.348 | 1.811 | 2.427 | 2.243 | 4.322 | 5.743 | 7.612 | 10.062 | 13.267 | 17.449 |

*n* = number of years

Source: Arthur J. Keown, *Personal Finance*, pg. 600.

The first column lists the number of years you intend to allow your investment to grow. The top row of percentages represents your expected rate of return. Go down to year thirty in the first column. Let's assume a very conservative growth rate of 6%. Now, move through the grid of numbers until you arrive at the column under 6%. You should arrive at 5.743. (I encased that number in a box to make it easier for you to find). That number is your *future value multiplier*. You simply multiply your initial investment ($10,000) by the future value multiplier (5.743). Your total should be $57,430. That $10,000 ring has the potential to cost you $57,430 in long-term savings. Now consider how much future money you stand to lose buying $30,000+ automobiles every few years!

That having been said, please do not call your fiancé and cancel the engagement. I simply want you to consider the very real long-term effects of large purchases. Perhaps you could settle for a $5,000 ring while investing the balance. That scenario would still net you a stunning diamond and leave you with $28,715 in thirty years! Get in the habit of thinking about what today's purchases will cost you many years from now, and it will change your mindset about the nature of money and affordability.

### The Time-Value of Money

One item often overlooked in the quest for personal wealth is the time-value of money. The time-value of money is a rather complex concept. Stated simply, the time-value of money is the reason that items seem to cost more over long periods of time. Perhaps your grandparents talk about a time when a soda was only 25 cents or a pack of gum just a nickel. My own great-grandparents enjoyed soda for only 5 cents and gum for a penny. Before the thought of 5-cent soda gets you excited, remember that our grandparents made less money for the same kinds of jobs that we do today. Due to inflation, a given amount of money will buy less and less over a long period of time. Of course, our salaries increase with inflation relative to the items we purchase.

What is important is that you understand what your money will be worth in *tomorrow's* dollars. Simply put, a $30,000 pile of cash today might buy a nicely appointed sedan. If you were to bury that $30,000 pile of cash in your back yard and dig it up 30 years from now, chances are it will buy much less automobile. In fact, you may only be able to afford tomorrow's equivalent of a current $20,000 car! So, why not run out and buy that car right now before your money loses value? Depreciation. You'll lose the value of your money anyway. Put the money in mutual funds, and compound interest will help your money grow instead.

In Chapter 5, we will discuss how to put the power of compound interest to work for your benefit. With careful planning, a solid financial future and comfortable retirement are well within your grasp. You might even be surprised how a small monthly investment can grow into a very substantial retirement fund.

# FROM A COMMODORE 64

April, 1984. I sat on the plush study carpet and watched in amazement as dad lifted the clamshell lid of the suitcase to reveal a small TV screen... and typewriter keys. I jumped up and down and shouted, "Dad bought us a computer!" He quickly doused my excitement by clarifying that he had just borrowed it from work for the weekend—bummer. Earlier that evening, dad had arrived home with a large and unusual suitcase. Apparently, he had taken this thing home from work. He could tell I was anxious to see what was inside and assured me we would open it up right after dinner.

Up to that day, I had only seen two computers; both were at the refinery where dad worked. I looked at computers as fun machines since I had played games on one of them and watched a funny little animated snowman on the other. Curious as to the purpose of this machine, I asked dad if we would be playing any computer games. Another difficult truth, according to dad, was that computers weren't for playing and that he had a project to work on. Still curious to see the machine working, I watched as the monitor warmed up and slowly revealed a glowing green prompt. In went a 5-1/2" floppy disk, followed by a kla-chunk as dad rotated the catch that locked the disk in place. After a brief series of clicks and whirs, green numbers appeared to spill down the screen. The trail of tumbling numbers seemed to scroll forever, ending abruptly with a blinking square cursor. I was staring at dad's first Lotus spreadsheet. More precisely, I was staring at dad's first automated financial plan.

Dad demonstrated to me how he broke down his income, taxes, and investments into columns. The rows represented pay periods out of which our family's expenses were tallied up and compared to income. He also explained how his income would likely increase over time and how that was figured into the program. I thought it was all very neat, but I was curious why he needed to go to the trouble of programing a computer for a thirty-year income projection. Why not figure it out one week at a time? At this point, I received another golden piece of advice. "Son, you need to plan ahead." He then revealed to me his lifelong goal: to retire a millionaire.

One million dollars! That sort of goal was almost as unimaginable to me as the concept of saving for a toy for three months. The only millionaires I had ever heard about were Richie Rich and Daddy Warbucks. It all seemed so impossible, yet so exciting at the same time. I may not have entirely understood *how* to get there, but from that day forward, I knew *I* wanted to retire a millionaire just like my dad!

# 5

# RETIREMENT SAVINGS

My parents retired. My grandparents retired. My great-grandparents retired, too. For most people, that line of reasoning leads to the conclusion that they will retire as well. On the whole, I think we take retirement for granted. As hard as it is to imagine, there was a time when the vast majority of people simply didn't retire. I'm not an economist. Neither am I a Wall Street stock broker. I don't have to be either one to see that America is in the grips of a retirement crisis.

While I hate to play Debbie Downer, the numbers are difficult to ignore. According to a 2018 report by the National Institute on Retirement Security, the median retirement account balance among all Americans is $0! Among those who have a retirement savings, the median balance at the time of the survey was only $40,000.[1] Those closest to retirement age were only showing amounts equal to or slightly greater than their own annual income. Spend any time in front of a television and you would be led to believe the exact opposite. There are advertisements the world over featuring retired couples enjoying fabulous lifestyles. Society is telling us that retirement is automatic and that a set of golf clubs and Alaskan cruise tickets just drop into our hands the day we turn 65. The reality, however, is that most middle-aged Americans aren't saving enough for retirement, and they are more likely to land in a state-run nursing home than a nice assisted-living facility. What concerns me the most is that it doesn't have to be that way. Any working American can retire comfortably with the right plan, hard work, and sacrifice. Furthermore, I believe that every American can retire a millionaire! This chapter will illustrate how any person of modest means can plan for a dignified retirement. I will also address some of the concerns, myths, and fears that new investors face when planning for retirement.

### Every American Can Retire a Millionaire

I lecture fairly often on radiology and radiation therapy-related topics. My audiences include X-ray students who are close to graduating and starting their first careers. When I look out over my audience, I can't help but see a room full of future millionaires. The typical radiologic technology student that pursues their degree immediately after high school can usually complete the program by age 23. Considering that minimum retirement age will likely be 70 by the time this year's class is ready to stop working, they'll have 47 years to save for retirement. That's 47 years of compound interest working its magic to ensure these young people a dignified existence in their golden years!

What, you might ask, makes me so sure that every American can retire a millionaire? After all, I've already admitted that I'm not an economist or stock broker. I know because of simple math. More importantly, I know because I was lucky enough to have a father who pointed me in the right direction by setting a great example. Growing up, I took for granted that my father's lessons were standard in every household. It was only in college that I discovered how few of my peers had received any financial guidance from their parents. I was surprised to hear my peers saying that becoming a millionaire was impossible and that it was pointless to even attempt. During those conversations, I often thought about the time when I was eight years old and dad showed me that retirement spreadsheet. I never doubted dad would reach his goal, and I never doubted that I would either (in spite of my missteps).

The problem with retirement savings and investing is that it's been so mystified. Many of my peers believe they need to have some special talent for "playing" the stock market. They don't believe they can save their way to a million dollars. Rather, they feel they have to buy into super-aggressive investments hoping to make large, quick gains, but instead they lose their shirts. The truth is, you don't have to be a banker, broker, or mathematician to become a successful investor. For that reason, I won't attempt to distract you with a bunch of fancy equations. Instead, we'll perform a simple exercise that will prove that pretty much any American can retire a millionaire.

As of this writing, the average American car payment for a new vehicle is $554.[2] That's according to Experian's State of the Automotive Finance Market Report for the fourth quarter of 2019. What if we were to drive a used vehicle we bought with cash instead? Now let's invest that average car note of $554 per month into a Roth IRA or 401(k) making a very conservative 6% interest. If you're the average X-ray tech, you'll be working from age 23 to 70 for a career span of 47 years. If you only invest the amount of money you are not spending on a car payment, you will retire with $1,400,000! Don't believe me? Type "retirement calculator" into your internet search bar. Put in these numbers. Planning a comfortable retirement is really that easy. Best of all, you have only thus far invested the difference of your car payment. This doesn't even count what you're contributing to your retirement at work or any match funds you may be receiving from your employer.

∿

## Retirement Vehicles

Your first retirement "vehicle" is your used, cash automobile. Once you've broken free of the chain of payments, you can turn your monetary resources toward a myriad of investment products. What should you choose? Again, retirement savings has been mystified to the point that many people are intimidated by it. Don't become distracted by smooth-talkers and naysayers. You can become a very successful investor utilizing the simplest of vehicles.

### *Employee-Sponsored Plan (401(k), 403(b), etc.)*

I start my investing right where I earn my salary by utilizing my employer's retirement plan. Perhaps you've heard of a 401(k) or 403(b). The numbers and letters, though confusing, don't mean all that much difference to your retirement. The 401(k) is designated for for-profit companies while the 403(b) is designated for non-profits. There are other types of employee-sponsored plans out there; these are just some of the most common ones. What's important is that you pay off your debt, save some emergency money, and then begin investing in whichever account is applicable as soon as possible. Most companies will offer what is called a *match* on your retirement contribution. My employer contributes 4% of my annual gross income regardless of how much I contribute myself. Most employers will match, dollar for dollar, the employee's contribution up to a certain point. For example, Rosie makes $50,000 per year. She contributes 15% of her gross income to her company's 401(k) plan, for an annual contribution of $7,500. Her employer matches up to 3% of her gross income, contributing an additional $1,500 per year. If a match is available from your employer, make sure you invest enough to qualify for the full amount—it's the closest thing to free money you'll ever receive!

Once you've signed on to your employer's 401(k) or 403(b), your money will be invested in groups of various stocks called *funds*. There are several types of funds: mutual funds (the most common), index funds, large-cap and small-cap funds. Some employer-sponsored plans allow you to move your money to different types of funds, while others allow less flexibility. If you want to take advantage of your employer's match, but you like the flexibility of moving your money around a wider array of funds, invest enough with your employer to receive your match and put the remainder into an IRA (individual retirement account).

### *IRA (Individual Retirement Account)*

The IRA is the DIY version of the 401(k) or 403(b). The IRA is not tied to your employer and it will allow you many more investment options. I've always had both an employer-sponsored plan and an IRA. When I've left employers in the past, I've taken the money from my employer-sponsored plan and moved it into my IRA (an action called a *rollover*). If I happen to receive a windfall in the form of cash, I generally put it in my IRA as well. Michele and I each have an employer-sponsored plan and an IRA.

### What Is a Roth IRA and When Is It Appropriate?

To answer the Roth question, we must fully understand the 401(k), 403(b), and IRA.

The traditional version of these investments allows pre-tax contributions; meaning, you don't pay taxes on the money when you place it in the account. Our friend Rosie placed $7,500 into her 401(k) in 2018. That $7,500 won't be counted in her taxable income for her 2018 tax year. However, she will be responsible for paying taxes on the interest she earns on that money when she cashes it out for retirement.

Enter the Roth. There is a Roth version of all three of our retirement account types. The Roth IRA, the Roth 401(k), and the Roth 403(b). The Roth version of each is *not* a pre-tax contribution; meaning, you will not reduce your taxable income by contributing to the account. At first, the Roth sounds like a bummer... but we're not quite done yet. When you cash out the Roth accounts at retirement, you pay no taxes on your withdrawals and no taxes on the interest you've accrued. If you're investing for 30 years, your account will consist mostly of interest.

The Roth is the preferred type of account for anyone who is still young and just starting out in their career. The traditional accounts are more likely to belong to older workers. It's possible to move money from a traditional IRA to a Roth IRA, or a traditional 401(k)/403(b) to a Roth; however, there are tax penalties for doing so. Remember, you don't pay taxes up front to contribute to a traditional account, and you don't pay taxes to pull money out of the Roth accounts. When rolling from traditional to Roth, you have to pay taxes somewhere, and you will pay them at the rollover. I know, because I made that very mistake. As a result, I switched financial advisors. I felt that my advisor should have warned me about the tax penalty when I rolled an old 401(k) into a Roth IRA. Fortunately, the mistake damaged my pride much more than my bank account. I hope I've helped you avoid making the same mistake.

### Retirement Do's and Don'ts

Your retirement plan can be as simple or as complex as you choose to make it. Retirement savings involves a large world of investment types and strategies that would be impossible to cover in this book. The good news is, if you're investing 15% of your annual gross income into your Roth IRA and/or your employer's Roth 401(k)/403(b), you are well on your way to retiring a millionaire. In the spirit of de-mysti-fying retirement and keeping things as simple as possible, I've compiled this easy list of retirement do's and don'ts that should get you started off on the right foot.

### *Do Start as Soon as Possible*

Every year you delay, you will lose compound interest. This is impor-tant because your account at retirement will contain exponentially less money each year that you fail to act. If you don't believe me, go back to the retirement calculator and plug in those numbers again. Only this time, change the numbers so that you are investing from age 47 to 75 (half the number of years as our first example). The result? You will now retire with $312,000. That's less than one-fourth of the 1.4 million dollars you would have accumulated in our previous example. Notice that you only halved the number of years you will be investing, but the end result is one-fourth the amount you would've had by starting twenty years earlier. It can almost be said that the power of compound interest works both ways. Take advantage of it early, and it acts like dynamite. Wait too long, and your retirement will turn out to be a dud.

### *Don't Think You Will Invest Later*

The best time to start saving for retirement is now. If you rack up a bunch of debt and live high on the pony today at the cost of your future, it will be more difficult to buckle down and initiate your retirement savings later. If you start off small with a beater car and slowly work your way up to something nicer, you will eventually have both a nice car and a strong retirement account. However, choosing to ignore your retirement and cruising around in a BMW could lead to an underfunded retirement account. At that point, you'll find it awfully difficult to climb back into a beater to get your finances under control.

If you're just starting out in your first career, start making contributions today that will put you into the millions by the time you retire. Build your budget around what is left. Your retirement contribution should inform your lifestyle, not the other way around! My dad said it best when I was growing up: "Send it straight from work to the bank so you don't miss it." If you are currently paying off debt, tackle it as soon as possible, then aggressively pursue your retirement goals.

### *Do Invest in a Roth*

If you have a Roth option at work, use it. If not, put enough in your account at work to receive your match, then start a Roth IRA. When it comes time to cash out for retirement, you'll be glad you did. If you're nearing retirement age and have traditional accounts, the Roth may not make sense for you. Please sit down with a trusted financial advisor before rolling funds from a traditional IRA to a Roth account.

### *Don't "Play" the Stock Market*

Sure, mutual funds are made of stocks, but they consist of a balance of stocks from many industries. Some stocks in the mutual fund portfolio may lose value, but others gain value and balance out the losses. Mutual funds have ups and downs just like company stocks, but they are far less risky. "Playing" the market requires that you constantly buy and sell stocks from specific companies in order to make quick, short-term gains. For regular folks like us, playing the market is more akin to gambling than investing. Unless you're a stock broker or day trader, there is really no reason to mess with stocks outside of mutual funds.

### *Do Utilize Dollar-Cost Averaging*

On the day you invest in your first mutual fund, you will have the option of receiving a check for your dividends (your interest earned) or reinvesting those dividends back into the mutual fund. Since compound interest depends on you reinvesting your dividends, that's exactly what you'll want to do. The interest you're earning on your IRA and 401(k)-type investments will automatically be reinvested. But what happens when the stock market dips and the value of your mutual funds goes down? Not to worry. Each time you put money into your account (i.e., make a contribution), you are taking advantage of dollar-cost averaging. Let's say you deposit $500 per month into an IRA that contains mutual funds. When the stock prices dip down (as they will certainly do), the overall value of your investments will decrease as well. However, your $500 investment will buy more stocks because the shares are now cheaper. Have you heard the phrase "buy low, sell high"? That's what dollar-cost averaging allows you to do. When the markets are up, your investments are worth more. When the markets dip down, you're buying stock at a lower price.

### *Don't Panic Anytime the Markets Dip*

Dogs bark. Horses neigh. Markets dip. It's what markets do. The markets will dip and your retirement fund values will go down. Those same markets will also bounce back, raising the value of your accounts. What's important to remember is that retirement savings is a long-term plan. Your funds will gain more value than they lose over 10, 20, and 30 years. If you panic and move your money around or cash out your non-retirement mutual funds every time there's an economic hiccup, you won't receive the benefits that long-term investing stands to offer. I've talked to many people who worry every time the DOW loses a few points. I've seen people cancel family vacations or put off home improvements because their investments lost value. Stocks and mutual funds are not the correct places to save for short-term goals. Keep your swimming pool money and vacation savings at your local bank. Keep only your long-term savings in stocks and mutual funds. Take advantage of the fact that the markets will gain value over the long run, and you won't have to worry about short-term economic blunders.

## Do Plan to Retire Only on Your Own Savings

When I first went to work in early 1999, one of the big talking points for the 2000 presidential election was what to do with Social Security. Many Americans felt that their benefits might not be there at retirement age. There are many folks who still feel that way. The political issues surrounding Social Security are best left to another book. All I really have to say is, better safe than sorry. The very first time I sat down with a financial advisor, I asked him not to include Social Security income in my retirement estimates. I wanted to be sure that I could become a millionaire all on my own. I suggest you do the same. If Social Security is still there when you retire, that's just *lagniappe* (pronounced lan-yap). Lagniappe is a Cajun term for "a little something extra."

## Don't Rely on Social Security or a Pension Plan

As I stated earlier, don't rely on anyone else to get you to your retirement goals. Social Security may or may not be there when you retire. Your company pension could be altered (or, like in some recent cases, lost) in a merger. Worst of all, you could wake up one day to find that your company's leadership perpetrated massive fraud and that your pension is non-existent. Don't rely on anyone but yourself. Fund your own way to a million dollars, and you never have to worry whether the fruits of your labor will be waiting for you at retirement.

## Retirement Naysayers

As with anything else you're doing right, there are bound to be Negative Nellies and Debbie Downers trying to drag you into their web of discontent. Remember, they are not giving you advice out of the kindness of their hearts; rather, they need you to fail so they don't have to feel alone. Here are just a few of the comments I've heard from individuals who love to justify not preparing for retirement.

### *You can't take it with you.*

You know what? You're absolutely right! I can't take my retirement account with me when I die. That's great news, too, because my family will need that money after I'm gone. You know what *you* can't take with you? All of the depreciating assets parked in your driveway! After you're gone, your family will have the distinct pleasure of having to take a loss on that Z-71 that's upside-down on payments while struggling to get rid of that custom golf cart for a fourth of what you paid for it. I wish you could take it all with you; your family would be better off without the burden.

### *Seize the day.*

I once thought I would "seize the day." Instead, I "seized the decade" and spent seven years paying off a Chevy Cavalier. If you really want to seize the day, seize the opportunity to take advantage of compound interest by investing your money instead of paying a car note.

*You could lose it all right before retirement.*

I've heard this one from individuals who are the same age as my parents. After the economic crash in 2008, millions of Baby Boomers did, in fact, lose very large portions of their retirement funds just a few years (or, in some cases, months) before they were supposed to retire. It was a terrible blow for far too many Americans. The media would have you believe that every single Baby Boomer was cheated out of retirement by that event. But I know that's not true. My dad didn't lose half his retirement. He didn't even lose one-third of it. In fact, he didn't postpone his retirement due to the market crash, either. Why is that? Like everything else "dad," his solution was simple: He wasn't invested in aggressive funds when the market crashed.

My father started young. He was investing in aggressive funds back in his 20s, 30s, and 40s. Sure, there were downturns during those years, too. The Black Monday crash of 1987 is a perfect example. Dad was only 41 at the time, which left his retirement funds plenty of time to recover from Black Monday and several other economic hurdles. By the time dad was in his late 50s, he could afford to switch to less aggressive investments. The less aggressive investments offered a higher tolerance for dips in the market. When dad could see retirement on the horizon, he had already shifted to low-risk investments. The economic calamity that cost so many Baby Boomers their retirements did little damage to those who had already moved over to low-risk investments.

This example once again illustrates the importance of starting young. My father's peers didn't lose their retirement funds because the stock market is evil or because Wall Street was out to get them. They lost their money because they were trying to make up for lost time by utilizing high-risk investments. If they had started younger, or had invested more money early on, they could have afforded to convert to less aggressive investments as they approached retirement. In many cases, dad's peers were living the good life in the 80s and 90s while dad was saving up and driving a paid-for brown Pinto. His decision to live modestly early on resulted in his being able to retire on his own terms. There is an important lesson to be learned here. Each and every monetary decision that you make has palpable ramifications on the future. Make wise decisions, and be ready to minimize your risk as you approach retirement. I promise that you will not "lose half of everything" the day before you are ready to stop working.

# GROW UP AND GET YOURSELF
# SOME DEBT

May, 1997. "You need to grow up and understand that debt is part of life," she demanded. We had been dating since September and the conversations about marriage were beginning to become more common. My girlfriend was ready to marry, settle down in the couple's dorm, and start a family. I thought it felt too rushed. After all, I would not be graduating for another 18 months; and her planned graduation date was at least two years away. I had no job or prospects. She was talking about leasing a car, and I'd never even had a credit card. When she brought up rent-to-own furniture, I nearly passed out! I hated the thought of making payments. She insisted that it was a man's duty to take on debt in order to provide for his family. After that conversation, I withdrew into a long cycle of thought and reflection. I ended the relationship because I felt our views on money and debt were just too different.

"Everybody is in debt." "Debt is normal." "You need to grow up and understand that debt is a part of life." I know for a fact that not *everyone* is in debt. I know many people, old and young alike, who are rejecting the "value" of debt in our society and living a cash lifestyle. And I am absolutely certain that our culture did not always rely so heavily on consumer debt. My grandparents never financed cars, clothing, or washing machines. They saved up cash money to build their modest homes (the keyword here is *modest*). I certainly can't regard debt as being "normal." After all, is it really "normal" to feel your back is against the wall every day for decades on end? Is it normal to feel like you're working long, irregular hours day after day only to mail away the fruits of your labor to an endless list of creditors? Sounds to me like desperation and servitude. The last time this many Americans felt trapped in desperation and servitude, we collectively revolted against the British.

# 6

# 'TILL DEBT DO US PART

A 2017 survey by Magnify Money revealed that one-third of participants earning over $100,000 named money problems as the root
cause of their divorce. Among those blaming money problems, 23%
reported debts of over $20,000. One-third of those surveyed indicated
overspending as the most persistent monetary issue.[1] Honestly, these
numbers don't surprise me. Between my own experience and that of
my friends and family members, I see more disagreements arise from
financial differences than from any other source. I've seen couples
spend behind each other's back, hide money from one another, and
use money as a tool for manipulation. Debt, spending, and selfish-
ness can easily force a good marriage into an uncontrollable death
spiral. That's why it is so important to choose your spouse wisely and
come to an agreement on money matters as soon as possible.

When two individuals are united in marriage, they become one.
Their assets and liabilities become one as well. A new couple
comprised of two individuals with little or no debt and lots of savings
will naturally have it easier than a new couple with little money and a
large pile of debt. The very best and most prepared couples will
struggle with the responsibilities of marriage and family; it takes

adjustment. Don't make things even more difficult by falling into financial distress. If you are currently married or considering marriage within a few years, please consider the following advice.

## Bring up Money ASAP

Determined to ward off potential problems, I often brought up money and budgeting on first dates. And yes, I'm sure that I scared off several women. Fortunately, Michele took a chance on me and the rest is history. I still remember revealing to her on our first date that I lived on a budget and that retirement savings and a "cash-only" lifestyle were important goals in my life. I even disclosed my salary to her and expressed to her the type of lifestyle she could expect if we were to enter into a successful relationship and marriage. Admittedly, I look back and realize my disclosure was probably too soon and too extreme. I don't actually recommend you start that way on a first date. I do, however, recommend you and your partner come to terms with financial habits long before the engagement.

## Savers and Spenders

You know the old cliché: "Opposites attract!" I wish I could say it was different for savers and spenders. I do know a few couples who are both natural-born savers, but they are few and far between. Most savers will marry individuals who spend more freely. Most spenders will marry someone who is more conservative with money. The good news is that this dynamic, if managed correctly, can lead to immense happiness for both the saver and spender (provided, of course, you are both willing to make reasonable compromises).

Such was the case with Michele and I. Before we met, Michele was more likely to buy items without a long-term plan and did not keep a written budget. She was a good saver of cash and had no credit debt, but she did not have a retirement plan in place. I, on the other hand, was a hopeless tightwad who didn't buy toilet paper without a comprehensive ten-page plan. Like my father, I always kept a written budget and had developed a long-term retirement strategy. I'm not saying I was better than Michele with money. After all, had I not met Michele, I probably would never have learned to enjoy myself. Had Michele not met me, she may not have learned to plan for the distant future. Very early on in our relationship, a very special transaction occurred between us. Michele gave me the gift of today. I gave Michele the gift of tomorrow. I loosened up and started taking short weekend excursions with Michele. Michele opened an IRA and began saving for retirement. We openly discussed our finances early on, and by the time we were engaged, we had developed a solid plan together.

At the time, we both carried debt. Michele had an SBA loan and I had some lingering student loans from LSU. We paid them off over a year before we got married. I'll never forget the night we celebrated our freedom from debt over a steak dinner. I was 36 years old at the time, and it was the first time I'd had dinner at a steak house! My point is, neither the spender nor the saver is "right." In many ways, the spender and saver need each other more than they know. In our case, Michele and I both experienced financial, personal, and spiritual growth as a result of our team effort and willingness to compromise.

The reconciliation of saver and spender does not come easy. There will be disagreements, frustrations, and down-right fights. Michele and I were no exception. This is why it's so vitally important to begin discussing finances as soon as possible. Unwillingness by either partner to broach the subject of finance is a valid concern for the future of the relationship and should be met with caution and careful consideration.

~

## Separate Accounts

The best way to guarantee that you and your spouse will never be on the same page financially is to utilize separate accounts. Think about it: Financial success occurs when you plan for the week, the month, the year, and beyond. This level of planning requires a written budget and a commitment by both partners to follow that budget. If you and your spouse are working out of separate checking and savings accounts, you can't even write a budget. How can you even be sure exactly what you make if you're not privy to your partner's income or spending habits?

So, why do couples often keep their money separate? I've heard many reasons and justifications, but I believe all of them can be boiled down to one simple idea: fear. Giving up unilateral control of one's income and spending can be frightening, especially for someone who is fiercely independent. The spender in the relationship often fears he or she will not have the freedom to do or own the things they have dreamed of. As a saver, I can attest to feeling a fear that the spender will take over and not leave enough to put away for the future. In a healthy marriage, couples discuss these feelings and reconcile them through understanding and compromise. Too many times, however, one or both partners insist on keeping the money separate so their previous habits may continue unhindered.

## It's Just Business

I am a hopeless, helpless romantic. You might then be surprised to know that I consider marriage to be a business. Michele and I are business partners. Each of us manufactures a net income. Some of that net income is reinvested into the business (retirement). Other monies are used to pay for the day-to-day operation of our business (household expenses). The remaining profits may be divided up to do as we please (disposable income). Every year, we review our net assets and liabilities to calculate our net worth. We judge our success by utilizing the same financial metrics as any large company. How can a romantic like myself possibly boil marriage down to a series of cold, calculated business transactions? Easy. I keep the money and love separate.

Marriage is a business. Marriage is also an expression of committed love and devotion. Business is cold and robotic. Love is warm and precious. The key to succeeding at both simultaneously is to not let them interfere with one another. Remember the old saying about not mixing business and pleasure, right? My point is that decisions made on the business end of the marriage (budget, retirement, savings, etc.) should never be carried into the amorous part of the marriage, and vice versa.

Let's say you and your spouse reach an uneasy compromise about how to utilize a bonus check. Maybe you didn't end up saving, spending, investing, or donating as much as you originally hoped or budgeted. It's okay! The important thing is that the two of you discussed it, came to an agreement together, and acted on the plan. If you keep doing that, the two of you will achieve your goals and more. What's most important is to continue moving forward after the decisions are made. Don't hold it against your spouse or bring it up as leverage in your amorous relationship, or in future decisions.

If you are not yet married, this is another great opportunity to remind you of the importance of discussing money with your significant other long before the wedding. A person who can't separate the business and amorous components of a relationship will likely show signs as soon as the relationship becomes serious. If you find yourself with someone who is using affection to manipulate financial decisions or vice versa, please reconsider the relationship or seek counseling.

## Mutually Assured Financial Destruction

There is a nasty habit that I see ruining marriages all around me.

I call it *mutually assured financial destruction*. You've probably seen the scenario play out among your friends or family as well. It involves a couple going quid pro quo on purchases (usually unnecessary ones) until the money runs out. Let's say a woman would like to purchase a $500 purse. Her husband would rather not spend the money on said accessary but would like a new $500 shotgun for himself. He offers to "allow" his wife to purchase the purse but only on the condition that he's allowed to purchase a shotgun. If you are in the wife's shoes, your new purse now costs $1,000. In the husband's case, that shotgun will cost $1,000. In most cases, the couple has only enough money to purchase one of the items while the other ends up on credit.

I was never one to give into a quid pro quo spending situation. I simply couldn't stomach the thought of everything I wanted costing twice as much. Michele and I have had these discussions, and it always results in neither one of us buying anything. Instead, we decide to be content with what we have and save our money. During those times that we have enough cash to both buy something special, we enjoy our purchases together as fruits of our collective toil.

For couples who are drawn into the fray, a never-ending vortex of spending awaits. If every time one spouse wants to make a purchase the other must make a purchase of equal value, they mutually assure that little or no money will be left for emergencies or savings. Believe it or not, I have seen this scenario played out in dozens of marriages, with most of them ending in divorce. Choose your partner carefully and discuss finances before making a deep commitment. Understand that differences in financial opinions are normal, and they can be overcome with compassion and communication. Don't hold back affection to manipulate a financial resolution with your partner, and don't use finances to manipulate an amorous resolution. Don't engage in quid pro quo spending and, most importantly, work with combined resources!

# A CAVALIER ATTITUDE

May, 1999. Six months into my non-profit career and life was looking great. I was a rising star, posting 10% growth in recruiting and participation. To that point, I had made fairly wise decisions with my money. My emergency fund was stocked and my retirement savings system was up and running. The months of long hours had left me weary, and there was an emptiness growing within. I had, for many weeks, been test-driving cars. I knew I was not ready to buy, but impatience was getting the better of me. I sometimes even sparred with the salesmen for practice because I saw myself as smarter and more car-savvy than the dealers. Little did I know my arrogance would land me in a financial quagmire one-decade deep.

The local Chevrolet dealership in town happened to be the hub of the largest chain of Chevy dealerships in the Southeastern United States. Just one week before, I had walked away from a deal on a Geo Tracker (a jeep-like vehicle built by Suzuki and sold by General Motors). At $11,000 slightly used, it was a steal compared to the Jeep Wrangler I was eyeing earlier that day. Too focused on negotiating the payments, I walked out of the deal over a difference of $25/month. I was fresh off the busted Geo deal and feeling confident I could handle another negotiation. I returned a week later to look at a Jeep Wrangler on the used car lot. The Jeep turned out to have far too many miles for the price, so I sauntered away hoping not to be approached by a salesman. And then I saw it: black-on-tan interior with snowflake wheels and gold accents! I didn't even like Chevy Cavaliers, but this one was just so... special. A Z-24 convertible that somehow reminded me of the black Trans Am from *Smokey and the Bandit* beckoned me forth. I was putty in this car's hands!

In a matter of moments, I was test-driving a car I hadn't even been looking for just 30 minutes before. I might have walked away from that Geo Tracker a week before, but this time would be different. After all, these guys were specialists in separating young men from their money. There was a large military base only minutes away, and new salesmen learned the art of pushing overpriced vehicles onto young GI's fresh out of high school. I wouldn't be getting the new guy this time. The friendly test-drive associate turned me over to the sales and finance guys.

Twice I attempted to leave the table. Twice the door was blocked while the "mouth" of the group beckoned me back down. First, I thought about the student-loan payment that had not yet begun to come due. The mouth assured me that their "rubric" proved I could afford the car. Second, I expressed concern over the increase in car insurance. After all, I was trading a bottom-of-the-barrel Toyota Tercel for a sporty convertible. Once again, two burly guys blocked the door while the mouth got in touch with his "insurance guy." By nine-thirty that evening, I was the proud lessee of a '99 Cavalier Z24 Convertible. Wait, did I say *proud*? I exited the sales cubicle well after closing time to thunderous applause courtesy of the sales staff. An old-fashioned balloon and ribbon drop finished off the effect. It was all designed to make me feel like a winner. Instead, I was completely terrified.

The next morning at work (after the most sleepless night of my life), I was smacked on the back and congratulated over my "purchase." Apparently, my coworkers didn't share my concerns. My supervisor leaned in and told me something that I had never heard before: "Don't worry about it, Chris, you'll always have a car note. Just think of it as a cost of doing business." I shot back, "That's silly, my dad never had a..." I stopped mid-sentence when I realized I had ignored one of the most important lessons I had learned from my father. As disciplined as I had been about retirement saving and budgeting, I'd let my emotions about an automobile dictate my actions and allowed the sharks to strike.

My car insurance increased just as I predicted, and my student-loan payments eventually came due. After that, my money situation went from manageable to very tight. Looking back, I could have done so much with that $279/month lease payment. I could have made four student-loan payments per month and been out of debt in under 18 months. Instead, I increased my debt by five-fold and spent 10 years cleaning up the mess! Had I paid off those student loans early and invested only half the payments thereafter, I would be so much closer to my retirement goals!

# 7

# THE DEALER ALWAYS WINS

The number one lesson to learn about car buying is that, like a Las Vegas casino, the dealer always wins. There is no such thing as a "great" or even a "good" deal. There are huge profits built into the price of automobiles. Even the so-called "dealer invoice" price has been padded to make you believe you're negotiating effectively. If you have paid dealer invoice, you have failed miserably!

Even worse off are the poor souls who return from the dealership extolling the virtues of their sales associate. "The salesman *really* worked with us and got that note right where we could afford it." I was in that group, by the way. "Getting the note where you can afford it" is dealer-speak for stretching out the term and raising the interest rate. There are two major problems with this. First, multiplying the monthly payment times the number of months and then adding TT&L (tax, title, and license) often results in a number much larger than the car's sticker price. In the case of the really unscrupulous dealers, the difference cannot be totally accounted for in taxes and interest payments. Sometimes they just sneak the profits back in because they catch the buyer not looking. The second problem is depreciation. "Helping" you into that shiny new car may involve the dealership stretching the note out so far that you will likely never catch up with your vehicles' depreciation rate. I know this is possible because it happened with the Cavalier. Allow me to illustrate.

I leased a 1999 Cavalier for $279/month. The payment assumed a vehicle value of $19,000 with a predicted residual value of $11,000. The *residual value* is what is sometimes referred to as the "balloon payment." (In other words, it's what they think the car's value will be at the end of your lease term.) General Motors, of course, overestimated the residual value by $3,500. At the end of the lease term, I was left owing $11,000 on a car that was worth only $7,500. I could not turn in the car, as I was way over on the mileage limit (another big mistake), and walking away meant fees high enough to wipe out my savings. Feeling like there was little alternative, I financed the balloon payment on a four-year term. (Yes, I took out an $11,000 loan on a $7,500 car.) Every month, I paid faithfully toward the balance, and every month the car's value continued to plummet. In late 2006, six months before I paid off the car, I still owed about $1,200. The car's value was $1,250. I had been upside-down on that car for nearly seven years!

## Car Poor

I must have *really* hated that car, right? Yes and no. I had tons of fun driving that convertible. In the ten years I drove that car, I can honestly say I had the top down more than half the time. The major issue was that it was the *only* fun I was able to have. By taking on a lease payment, I made myself car poor. My convertible was cool and fun, but at the end of the month, I had no money to *do* anything. During the time I drove the Cavalier, I couldn't afford to participate in the many other hobbies I had enjoyed before. In many ways, my convertible felt like its own type of prison. I find this ironic since Americans associate their automobiles with freedom and mobility.

The first question you should ask before any car purchase is: "Do

I have enough cash on hand to buy this car?" If the answer is no, you cannot afford the car! Unfortunately, car leases have become so prevalent that many personal finance textbooks entertain the mathematics for the purpose of comparison to traditional car ownership. I will simply tell you that leasing a car is stupid! I know because I've done it myself. Think about it. Would you go to Enterprise or Hertz and ask to rent a car for three years? Of course not. That is essentially what you are doing when you chose to lease a vehicle. And, in most cases, you get the added bonus of having to pay for maintenance— even Hertz and Enterprise won't make you do that!

## Car Leases Are a Farce

Even a personal finance textbook will tell you that car leases are designed to allow you to drive more car than you could normally afford. Of course, that reasoning assumes you were going to make loan payments on a lesser car. Wait a minute... if you were going to make payments, you can't afford the lesser car in the first place. To lease something even more expensive means you extremely-super-double cannot afford it!

Before I understood the mechanics of leasing or the sheer number of leases issued per capita, I felt jealous of individuals driving really nice cars. According to a 2017 report by Edmunds.com, leases accounted for a record 31% of new car sales in 2016.[1] One out of every three luxury cars you see on the road is leased, which means the driver likely cannot afford it. Kind of takes the jealousy out of the equation, right?

Yet, our car-obsessed culture praises the automobile as a symbol of wealth, success, and freedom. Nothing could be further from the truth! Automobiles strip you of your wealth while consuming an average of $550 per month in payments. Gone are the traditional three and four-year loan terms. The Consumer Financial Protection Bureau reports that a staggering 42% of new car purchases now carry terms of six years or more.[2] Those payments, carefully invested, could have added up to millions of dollars over your working life. As for being a symbol of success, there is no greater success in my world than being prepared for emergencies, college, and retirement without having to worry where the money will come from. Consider this: Mercedes, BMW, Lexus, Infinity, and Acura will lease a car to just about anyone with a pulse. How can these marks represent *true* success if nearly anyone can attain them? A farce, indeed.

What about the idea that the automobile represents freedom? I have never been freer than when I decided to stop making car payments! When you're making a $550 per month payment on a vehicle, are you *free* to do whatever you want? Before you say yes, think of the times you had to make tough decisions at the end of the month. You have likely had to say no to *something* you or a family member wanted to do or buy. Maybe you said yes and swiped a credit card for that item. Eventually, the bill comes due and you will inevitably have to make difficult choices.

If you would have seen me on the road in 1999, top down and hair floating in the wind, you might have thought I was wild and living free. The reality of my situation was very different. I was so car poor that I was living on $70-$100 per month of groceries. I could not afford to upgrade my 9" television, and cable was out of the question. I should have spent my time in Georgia exploring the outdoors through hiking, kayaking, and whitewater rafting. Instead, I sat in my apartment every weekend staring at my black and gold "ticket to freedom."

## Common Car-Buying Myths

As the cost of new vehicle ownership steadily rises, the payments and terms continue to grow. In order to justify $550+ payments per month on 72-month terms, society has developed some very popular automotive myths aimed at keeping you a slave to the monthly car note. I hope that, by dispelling these myths, you might be inspired to break the car-note habit for good!

### You will always have a car note.

A few months after leasing the Cavalier convertible, I finally confided in my supervisor the nature of my financial woes. Attempting to offer encouragement, he patted me on the shoulder and said, "Cheer up. After all, you will always have a car note." My immediate thought was "NO! My dad didn't *always* have a car note, more like *never* had a car note." My plan was to pay this thing off at some point and not have a car note for at least a few years. Before I could complete that thought, my supervisor added, "No use to keep driving them after they're paid off cause they'll be out of warranty by then." Although I don't like the idea of making payments on a car that is out of warranty, I wouldn't get rid of one for that reason alone. The truth is, you don't have to always have a car note. You can choose to *never* have a car note. I have done both, and I can attest that the joy of *never* paying a car note far surpasses that of *always* having a car note.

### A car is just a cost of doing business.

This was another pearl of automotive wisdom courtesy of my first supervisor. His theory followed that a car transports you to work and is, therefore, a work expense. If that were true, the IRS would allow us to claim our personal vehicles as tax write-offs. The truth is that cars are an expense, and any businessman worth his salt seeks to reduce expenses while increasing revenues. If a personal vehicle were equivalent to a business expense, said businessman/car owner would seek to own a vehicle at the least possible expense. For me, that always means a reliable used car purchased with cash. My supervisor's V8 Grand Cherokee was definitely *not* the best way to lower business expenses!

### *A new car is safer and more reliable.*

I dropped by the local Honda dealership once to grab transmission fluid for my Accord. Six salesman immediately descended upon my car thinking I was there to make a trade. The most persistent of the bunch followed me all the way to the parts counter making trade-in offers. He told me I should get into a "safer" and "more reliable" Honda. My car was an '03 and this was sometime around 2013. Personally, I didn't feel my car was unsafe or unreliable. The "safer and more reliable" argument could be made when comparing modern vehicles to those built, let's say, before 1990. Any vehicle built after that, however, benefits from fuel injection, air bags, and antilock brakes. Cars with these features are certainly safe and reasonably reliable. To state that a modern 10-year-old car is unsafe and unreliable is to say that 10 years ago I was in grave danger of dying or breaking down every time I got behind the wheel. Once again, this myth just doesn't stand up to scrutiny.

### *Once you own a car, the next one always has to be nicer and more expensive.*

There was a short time in between non-profit administration and civil drafting that I worked as an inside salesman at a gasket factory. The pay was low and the work was unfulfilling, but it motivated me toward longing for something better in life. I befriended a young lady at the gasket factory who worked in purchasing. She was very young and newly married with a small child. Her husband worked in the meat department at a local grocery chain. I don't think either one of them had completed high school. I was surprised then to see her pull up to work in a brand-new Mitsubishi Eclipse Turbo Convertible. Knowing how I struggled with the lease on my own car, I knew they must have been buried in payments. After all, her husband had a new truck and they had recently purchased a home. I chose not to press the issue with her; it was really none of my business anyway. I complemented her on her purchase and went about my day.

A few months later, we were talking cars in the breakroom. She confided in me that she was having a really tough time with the note but that she really had no choice but to go with a "better" car. She had been driving a small Toyota for several years and decided it was time to upgrade. Instead of making her decision based on family finances, she went straight to a nicer car. Her reasoning was that *you can't go backwards in cars; you always have to get something better.* I managed to keep a straight face while internally I was yelling "NOOOOOO!" My dad never upgraded automobiles. Everything he ever drove was bottom-trim with manual locks, windows, seats, and vinyl upholstery. Once, in 1985, he purchased a car for mom that happened to have a cassette player in it. My sister and I thought we were the Rockefellers!

The idea that you must upgrade with every car purchase is yet another cobblestone on the road to financial ruin. Most Americans replace their vehicles every five to seven years. If you were to go from Pinto to Chevy to BMW in 15 years, your spending would surely outpace any raises you received during that time frame. The only path to vehicular upgrades is founded on how much cash you have saved for your next vehicle.

## When to Buy

As long as you have a reliable vehicle, there is no real *need* for car shopping. If, however, your current vehicle is totaled in an accident or requires a repair costing more than the car's value, another vehicle may be considered. That is, of course, if you have the cash available.

Again, I cannot stress enough the importance of having an emergency account. Most financial advisors and money gurus suggest stockpiling 3-6 months of take-home pay for just such emergencies. For the sake of argument, let's pretend that you have an emergency fund, are saving for retirement, putting away money for the kid's college, and have no other debts besides your mortgage. You have about $10,000 saved towards your next vehicle and your current vehicle is at the end of its rope. Guess what? You are in the perfect position to purchase a really nice used car!

Instead of putting that $10,000 down on a new vehicle and settling for a car note, try purchasing a reliable used vehicle. You might be surprised by what your $10,000 will buy.

It may take a little more research and a little know-how, but a great vehicle can be had for $10,000. I know because Michele and I were recently in a similar situation. In our case, it was my stepdaughter's car that was at the end of its rope. Instead of purchasing a car for her, I gave her the Accord Coupe I had purchased with cash eight years earlier. During those years without a car note, Michele and I were able to save about $15,000 (aside from our retirement, emergency fund, etc.). We just called it the car account and decided to add to it until we absolutely had no other choice but to purchase a vehicle.

In March of 2018, my stepdaughter's Toyota Avalon had become too expensive to continue dumping money into. Michele and I began shopping for our next vehicle—a used Toyota 4Runner. To make a long story short, we were able to find an older, low-mileage 4Runner for right at $10,000. The vehicle was in great condition cosmetically and mechanically. As a bonus, it was complete with all service records. With cash in hand, we were able to negotiate the $12,500 asking price down to $10,000. With tax, title, and license fees, the total came up to about $11,000. This left us with a $4,000 head start on our next vehicle. And best of all, we walked out title in hand with no payments whatsoever!

The question of when to buy a vehicle comes down to preparedness and priorities. First, do you have your priorities in order? Are you debt-free, save the mortgage? Are you contributing enough to your retirement and/or college savings to hit your target goals (in this case, fully funding your children's college education and retiring with a one-million-dollar net worth)? Do you have 3-6 months of take-home pay saved up? If you have answered "yes" to all of these questions, congratulations! You are prepared to make a cash car purchase. If your purchase is the result of an unexpected event, such as a breakdown or accident, dip into your emergency money. If you have a separate account just for saving up for a nice vehicle, you are in total control of your finances!

### Always Buy Used (and Ignore the Naysayers)

You are in command of your financial destiny and ready to purchase a reliable cash vehicle. Beware the naysayers; they will be quick to profess upon you the classic myths concerning used cars.

*When you buy used cars, you're just buying other people's problems.*

There might have been some truth to that myth many years ago when the usable life span of an automobile was 10 years or 100,000 miles. Plastic and rubber components have gotten much better and last longer. Modern roads are generally better, too, and don't punish vehicles the way they did when this myth was first established. Modern cars are routinely staying on the road for 20+ years and racking up 250,000–300,000 miles. My experience has been that a 10-year-old vehicle with 100,000 miles on the odometer is just getting broken in!

*Don't ever buy a used car 'cause it has no warranty.*

Suppose that used car drops a starter or needs an alternator right after you drive it home? The fact that you paid cash for the car takes care of that. You have control of your financial life; therefore, you have the funds to pay cash for a new part. Yes, it's frustrating to replace a part on a vehicle you just purchased. Is it better than having to pay a car note? You bet it is! When you buy a used car and pay cash, you are self-warranted against breakdowns. You've been saving the $550 per month that your peers are mailing to General Motors Financial Services, so you have the $150 for a new starter or alternator. Buying a new car only for a warranty is just as dumb as buying extended warranties on any consumer product. It's always better to save your money and become your own extended warranty.

## Beat Depreciation

The number one deterrent for buying new is depreciation. We have all heard that new cars lose 20% or more of their value as soon as you drive them off the lot. There is only one other way to lose money more efficiently: pile it up in your yard and set it on fire! So why do people continue to voluntarily light their money ablaze? I think that most people just don't run the numbers. Let's say you purchase a brand-new $20,000 vehicle and put down $5,000. By the time you reach your driveway, that car is now worth $15,000. You basically paid $5,000 to drive your car home... once.

And what about the year or two that you spent saving up that $5,000 down payment? That sacrifice has vanished; you will never get that back. The situation is even worse if you put down less money. Let's say you only have $2,500 for a down payment. You still owe $17,500 plus tax, title, license, and interest. Assuming 10% tax and 5% interest on a five-year term, you arrive home that evening owing a total of $21,565 for a car that is worth only $15,000! Congratulations! You are officially upside down on your car! Get accustomed to it, you may not be able to pay it off faster than it's depreciating. In fact, the picture gets even bleaker as your vehicle reaches two and three years of age. By then, the car that you cherish so much—the one you wash, wax, and meticulously maintain—has now lost a stunning 50% of its initial value! Think you can stop the bleeding with a new set of wheels and a stereo? Think again. Everything you add to that vehicle will lose value right along with it.

When you buy a used car, you are allowing someone else to take that 20% loss for you. By the time you take that three-to-five-year-old car home, it's rate of depreciation has slowed drastically. Instead of losing 20% upon purchase, you are more likely to lose only 5-10% per year (depending on the make and model). Yes, your used vehicle will depreciate, too. However, the loss will be substantially less (and slower) than that of a new vehicle.

Before my financial awakening, I believed it was about the same financially to buy a new car and drive it for 20 years as it was to buy two used vehicles and drive them each for ten. Deep down, I must have known I was mistaken because I avoided doing the math. Now that I have experience with used vehicles, I can attest through my own experience (with real-world numbers) that used beats new every time!

In 2010, I bought a 2003 Honda Accord from a coworker. I paid $8,000 cash for that car, which had about 90,000 miles on the odometer. I drove that car for eight years and then gave it to my step-daughter, who owned it for eighteen months. By the time she sold it, it had been in the family for ten years. That means I basically paid $800 per year for that car! I can take the math one step further. She sold the car for $2,700. If we subtract that amount from the original purchase price, we drove that Accord for ten years at a cost of $5,300 ($530 per year)! The year that I bought the Accord, I had test-driven a brand-new one of the same trim level. That car stickered for $23,000 in 2010. If I had bought that car and driven it ten years, it would have cost $2,300 per year. How long would I have had to drive it for it to cost only $530 per year? 43 YEARS! Which vehicle do you think represents the better value? I believe I will fair out even better with the 4Runner. 20-year-old 4Runners with 250,000 miles can be found on CarGurus for around $5,000. If the value of my 4Runner follows suit, I might end up driving this $10,000 vehicle for 10 years before selling it for $5,000. That would put my yearly cost at $500. Used cars win every time!

## Research Your Purchase

Hopefully, I have convinced you that buying used is the best way to go. Now it's time to research your purchase! Buying a used car requires much more careful research than buying new. The good news is, there is much more data out there related to the used car you are interested in. How is that so? Brand-new cars have yet to hit the road in numbers; therefore, there is little information available as to their long-term reliability. This is especially true of models that have undergone major design changes for the new model year.

Would you be surprised to know that, even though my father purchased his vehicles new, he never bought a vehicle within two years of a redesign? His reasoning was that redesigned models were destined to have some flaws which would need to be worked out over the following year or two. It shouldn't surprise you then that my father has owned several ultra-reliable vehicles that have given 15+years of dependable service. When buying a model that has been on the road for five to ten years, there is mounds of data available on that vehicle's long-term reliability, as well as quirks specific to its model year. You just have to know where to look. If you're tired of handing your hard-earned money over to mechanics and dealerships, or you simply want to learn more about the inner-workings of your vehicle, there are boundless resources available for learning about basic car maintenance.

### *Automotive Forums*

The internet is an outstanding source of information when

researching a car purchase. Just about every make and model of automobile has a fan following. This is true for cars as gorgeous as the latest BMW to ones as ugly as the AMC Gremlin. Whatever you are interested in driving, there is sure to be an internet forum for that specific vehicle and year model. Forums are a great place to begin your research because they offer a sneak-peak at a vehicle's reliability, engineering faults, and quirks. The individuals participating in the forums are often there to give each other advice on repairs, so they seldom pull punches when it comes to critiquing a vehicle's engineering.

Automotive forums usually contain a "how-to" forum with instructions on performing basic maintenance and minor (and sometimes major) repairs. I never purchase a vehicle without spending time on a forum related to the particular make and model I'm considering. Automotive forums are full of information that can help you diagnose and solve many minor problems that could otherwise cost hundreds of dollars. I once had a safety switch fail on the Honda that was preventing me from putting the car in drive. An unscrupulous dealership or mechanic could have told me my transmission was bad and hit me with a $5,000 repair, and I would have been none the wiser. A quick trip to the Honda forum steered me toward an $8.00 switch that took five minutes to replace. I can't count how many single moms I've seen with similar problems who ended up buying a new car they couldn't afford simply because the dealership took advantage of their lack of knowledge! Forums are a great place to get to know your car, and the members will typically warn you of the most crooked dealerships in your area.

### Shop Manuals

The very first purchase I make after buying a used automobile is a shop manual. You can find shop manuals for most cars and trucks at any auto-parts retailer. If you're super frugal, you can buy them for cheap at a used online bookstore. Your local library may stock shop manuals as well. Shop manuals tend to offer more in-depth details concerning maintenance and repairs on your vehicle. Even if you only use the shop manual to study a repair and conclude that it's over your head, you at least have made yourself more familiar with your vehicle. The more familiar you are with your vehicle, the less likely it is that a mechanic or dealer can take advantage of you. Remember, crooked mechanics and dealers can smell someone who lacks automotive knowledge, and they know when and where to strike at your wallet. If they even sense you have some idea of how your car operates, they probably won't risk shooting you a line of bull!

## Consumer Reports

Another outstanding source of automotive research is *Consumer Reports* magazine. You can typically pick up a copy of their annual new car reliability reports at any bookstore. (That's right, I said *new* car). *Consumer Reports* considers the reliability of past models to make predictions on the reliability of new models. If a particular model in the report's line-up is highly rated, it has typically enjoyed a long history of above-average reliability. *Consumer Reports* will even include reliability information on trim/engine/transmission configurations that are more troublesome than others for one particular model.

## Ask an Honest Mechanic

If you are fortunate enough to have an honest, trusted mechanic, seek their advice as well. A good mechanic can tell you which vehicles they see for repair most often and what type of repairs those vehicles require. I've had mechanics turn me away from certain engine/transmission combinations in some cars due to premature failures they have seen in the shop. Mechanics are also in tune as to which vehicles often require repairs so expensive that the vehicle is rendered a total loss. You might be surprised to know that there are some 5- and 6-year-old cars out there dropping transmissions that cost more than the car is worth to repair. A good mechanic will steer you clear of those models!

## Always Pay Cash

The best deals I've ever made were on used vehicles purchased with cash. Buying with cash is easy on you and easy on the seller, too. You will always have the upper hand when paying with cash because you won't have to wait on a loan approval. The best part of a cash deal is that you walk away with a title and no payments. Aside from lowering the negotiated price, cash payment offers two other major financial benefits: lower taxes and zero interest.

When Michele and I purchased our 4Runner, we negotiated the $12,500 sticker price down to $10,000. With a Louisiana State sales tax rate of 10%, that $2,500 difference equates to a tax savings of $250. Assuming we had taken out a $10,000 loan for 36 months at 5%, we would have racked up over $750 in interest payments. Paying with cash saved us over $1,000 just on taxes and interest fees. Just imagine how much you could save by paying cash for a $20,000 or $30,000 vehicle.

## Beware the Naysayers

One of the best ways to save measurable dollars is to perform your own basic car maintenance. To many of you, especially those not raised working on automobiles, the prospect may sound quite intimidating. That's exactly how manufacturers and dealerships want you to feel! In fact, there are several myths concerning DIY car repair that are designed especially to keep you out from under the hood of your car.

### *"Everything's computerized and you can't work on them anymore."*

Wouldn't the dealerships love to see you read that and give up? The truth is, computers have taken over some of the mechanical components of your engine that used to set timing and meter out fuel. Those parts used to require a great deal of maintenance. Now, those maintenance items no longer exist. It's not that you "can't work on them anymore;" rather, you don't have to work on them nearly as much as you used to. When problems do strike your car's fuel, timing, or ignition systems, it is typically due to failed sensors (not the computer itself). These problems typically cause the dreaded "check engine" light. Fortunately, the fault that is causing the light can be diagnosed free-of-charge at most auto-parts retailers! I'm serious! Take your car to an O'Reilly's, AutoZone, or Advance Auto Parts store (the predominate store in your region may differ). Let them know you have a check engine light and need your codes pulled. Within minutes, they will be able to point you in the right direction. Sometimes, the root cause of the problem will require intervention by a mechanic. Most of the time, it will only be a matter of replacing a sensor.

### *"They'll void the warranty if you work on it."*

Correction: Some manufacturers will void your warranty if you make modifications to the vehicle. Maintenance and repair don't fall into this category. If you are following my advice, you are buying a used car for cash, so the warranty is probably irrelevant. If your vehicle happens to be under factory warranty, don't jack it up, reprogram the computer, or install a "high performance" exhaust. Those items may void your warranty. The exhaust system will make your car sound like a mechanical wet fart, so just avoid that altogether.

## Driving a Beater is so Much Sweeter!

What if you chose *not* to write off your paycheck to everyone else every month? You could actually afford to go out and do things you enjoy. More importantly, that $550 per month you are *not* mailing away to General Motors Financial Services could fund a really comfortable retirement! My first "beater" was the 2003 Honda Accord Coupe that I bought for cash in 2010. Some people may find their beater takes the form of a minivan or SUV. Whatever the case, there is no other lifestyle choice that will give you more "bang for the buck" in regards to your finances than a paid-for vehicle. When you buy a vehicle used, someone else takes that 20% (or more) hit in value, plus additional losses due to mileage and wear. By the time you buy that vehicle used, it costs thousands less and will save you thousands more on taxes and interest. There is simply no better way to build wealth, enjoy life, and save for the future than by owning used, cash cars.

# GIVE ME SOME CREDIT (SCORES)

When I bring up financial responsibility, so many people like to open the discussion by touting their high credit score. The debt-laden masses continue to sing the praises of FICO as if it's the number one way to measure financial success. The truth is, the credit score wasn't discussed just 25 years ago. Go back a few more years, and you'll find a time when credit cards weren't even used very often. Better yet, pour a glass of wine and relax into your favorite chair as we travel to a glorious time in America's past when you could check out at a retail store and not be asked to sign up for a credit card. Psst. Don't get too comfortable... that part doesn't last very long.

Until the latter part of the 80s, credit cards were a pain to use. You had to hand the card to a clerk who then filled out a carbon tri-copy receipt before placing the card in a mechanical device. The clerk then manually moved a spring-loaded roller over the card, imprinting the card's number onto the receipt. The tri-copy was broken down into its three constituent parts; with one copy going to the store, one to the customer, and one to the credit card company. Sometimes it took months for your purchase to show on a statement. In the meantime, the receipts were often lost resulting in overspending. Believe it or not, using a credit card was more difficult and time consuming than paying cash!

All that changed after the advent of the magnetic strip. As more and more venues upgraded to card readers, the masses dove in to experience the ease and convenience of "swiping the card." Credit cards were marketed as a form of power. One's ability to flash a card and "make it happen" certainly fit the 80's mantra of "have it all, have it now." It wasn't long before retailers realized they were making almost as much money from their deals with the card companies as they were from their own merchandise. Retailers were quick to adapt by offering their own store-brand credit cards. The popularity of the credit card blossomed, and the idea of the credit score grew with it.

Personally, I had never heard of a credit score until the popular Freecreditreport.com commercials began airing in the early 2000s. This legendary ad campaign (that is still running in one form or another) featured a series of catchy tunes played by a down-and-out musician lamenting about the financial limitations imposed on him by his poor credit score. The underlying message? That a low (or no) credit score meant that you were impoverished with no hope of improving your station in life. A high credit score was equivalent to financial success and unlimited freedom. For those who grew up influenced by those ads, the credit score has been normalized as a necessary part of everyday life in America.

You can throw out the idea that you need a credit score! If you choose to pay cash for cars, clothing, appliances, vacations, and everything else, there is practically no need for a credit score. There are even mortgage lenders that will still arrange a home loan without a credit score. The "American dream" of home ownership shouldn't require you to use debt simply to prove that you can pay it back. You can show the bank that you are a low-risk borrower by demonstrating that you can budget, save, and invest responsibly.

# 8

# YOUR FIRST HOME

Your home will likely be the largest single purchase you will ever make. Unless you own other real estate, it will be your only appreciating material asset other than your investments. If that scares you, it should! A home can make or break you financially depending on the circumstances surrounding its purchase, so it pays to take your time and get it right. So many individuals in my generation were in such a rush to buy a home. I never understood the rush. I think that entitlement is partly to blame. My parents and many of their peers were raised in small homes. They dreamed of raising their own families in larger, nicer homes where their children would not have to share bedrooms.

My parents started their marriage in a small rental house and slowly worked their way up into the home they'd dreamed of since childhood. The children of my generation (Gen X) were the prime recipients of their hard work. We weren't around back when mom and dad were crammed in a tiny rental house scraping together collateral for a construction loan. The 1,800 square-foot homes many of us grew up in became our "small" childhood home and set us off dreaming of the 2,500 square-foot homes we hoped to occupy in

adulthood. There was only one problem: Many couples of my generation skipped right over the rental house part, then totally ignored the
collateral as well (or, in our case, down payment part).

Most of the people I grew up with jumped straight into that large
dream home fresh out of college. We felt a sense of entitlement to the
same comfortable standards we grew up with, and I believe that is a
large part of the reason my generation faces a retirement-savings
crisis. To make matters worse, many of my friends purchased their
large homes with adjustable rate, no-down-payment mortgages in the
middle of the housing boom. When the housing bubble burst in
2008, many of my friends were propelled into instant, massive *negative equity*. Luckily, I had avoided buying a home during that time and
was able to learn a few lessons by watching the housing crisis unfold.

### Know What You Can Afford

If you call a mortgage company to inquire about how much house
you can afford, you are already a calf marching into the slaughter-
house. Banks are very poor learners. In spite of everything that
happened in 2008, they will still loan you much more money than
you can comfortably afford to pay back. Notice I said "comfortably."
The bank might assure you that you can pay back a $400,000 home
loan, but they will never tell you that it will feel like 30 years of financial servitude!

Some personal finance textbooks will advise you to take out a
loan with a payment no greater than about 30% of your gross pay
(regardless of term). In my experience, that is still too much. Michele
and I are very comfortable and happy with our current payment,
which is based on 20% of our net pay. That's right, 1/5 of our *take-home*
pay. That leaves us with plenty of wiggle room for increases in property taxes and insurance. Personal finance expert Dave Ramsey
recommends a payment of no more than 25% of your take-home pay
on a 15-year fixed-rate mortgage, and I agree that your payment

should not be a penny more than that (inclusive of your insurance and taxes).

## Make the Largest Possible Down Payment

Your down payment can sometimes make the difference between a monthly note that is affordable to you, or just plain outrageous. Years ago, banks often required 10-20% down on all home purchases. Personally, I wish they still did. With the advent of the "special" no-down-payment mortgage, just about anyone with a pay stub and a pulse can get in over their head with a house they can barely afford. Large down payments are important because they reduce the amount of money you have to borrow in order to purchase your home.

For example, a $200,000 home mortgaged at 4% for 15 years with no down payment will generate a monthly note of $1,479 (not counting insurance, property tax, and PMI). PMI (private mortgage insurance) is a mandatory insurance applied to your monthly note when you have not put down at least 20% on your home purchase. Remember, PMI is not there to help you. You receive no benefit from having it; it's there to protect the bank's investment. PMI is like depreciation on a car. You might as well set fire to hundreds of dollars per month. With insurance, property tax, and PMI, your monthly payment on that $200,000 home will likely exceed $2,000 per month. By the end of the 15-year term, you will have paid $65,000 in interest.

Let's go through the same calculations with a 20% down payment. You put down $40,000 on a $200,000 home. You will now only pay interest on the remaining $160,000 you have financed. All other things being equal, your payment now drops to $1,184—a reduction of $295! You will also save $100-$200 per month on PMI! Who wouldn't want to spend $500 less per month? As an added bonus, your total interest payments are now $52,500—a savings of $12,500! A large down payment not only lowers your monthly note, it saves you thousands on interest and PMI charges. Better still, that large down payment will protect you from market fluctuations. With a large down payment, you are less likely to find yourself upside-down on your home if a temporary dip in the housing market should occur in your area.

## How Do I Save for a Down Payment?

Sure, I can talk about saving $40-60,000 for a down payment on a home, but how easy is it to amass that much cash? Honestly, it's not easy at all. Saving a large down payment or buying a home with cash requires a monumental commitment. It requires sacrifice and diligent budgeting. I will use the example of a couple making $65,000 per year gross income. The first 30% ($20,000) will go toward income taxes and Social Security payments and another 10% ($6,500) will go to their church. That leaves $38,000 per year to live on and save. We can break that down to about $3,200 per month.

Here's where very careful lifestyle planning comes into play. As you save for a home, it is very important that your rent not exceed one-fourth of your take-home pay. That limits you to an apartment or rental house costing no more than $800 per month. If you can manage to live off of only $1,400 of the remaining $2,400, you can save $1,000 per month! At that rate, you will have saved $40,000 in a little over three years. If you were to put that $40k down on a $140,000 home, your note will be right around $800 per month. Now you are in a home that you can easily afford with a payment no higher than your former rent. Even better, you will move into your new home with plenty of equity.

As I said before, saving that kind of cash is not easy. That's why it is so important that you not bury yourself in automotive, student, and credit card debt. The savings scenario I laid out earlier would be downright miserable (if not impossible) with a $500 car payment or a $10,000 credit card balance. If you have those debts, focus on paying them off as soon as possible. Then turn that money directly toward your down-payment savings. As a result of your lower note on a shorter term, you will be able to pay that house off quickly and have all of your income available to you for your enjoyment.

## Avoid Gimmicks

When the housing market is hot, the sharks start patrolling! Such was the case in 2003 when America was in the cusp of the housing bubble. The 9/11 terrorist attacks threatened to stifle the economy, causing the feds to hold interest rates low. It wasn't long before the American public, caught in a low-interest frenzy, began buying up real estate hand over fist. The hot market soon led to shorter supplies, creating a sharp rise in home values. Suddenly, millions of people completely unprepared to buy homes were signing up for any program that could "help" them take advantage of the market.

Anytime a financial institution expresses a desire to "help" you get into that dream home, their claim should be met with caution. Banks always seem to be coming up with some "new product" that will get you into that home that you "otherwise couldn't afford." I can promise you, they won't be so helpful come the day you can't make the payment. Such is the case with the HELOC (home equity line of credit) and the ARM (adjustable-rate mortgage).

When planning to buy a home, please be aware of these and other top banking gimmicks.

## Long-Term Mortgages

During the early days of the housing boom, circa 2002, my workplace was receiving fax advertisements for 99-year mortgages. That is an absolute no brainer. Run any online mortgage calculator and you will see that the monthly note isn't much better than that of a 30-year mortgage. That's primarily due to the insurmountable interest fees accrued over the length of the term. Speaking of interest, the 99-year loans are sometimes referred to as interest-only loans because you will practically never reach a point when you are paying towards your principle. After some research, I found that 99-year mortgages are exceedingly rare and only used in very specific markets. However, they have become quite normal in countries like Japan and Sweden.

If the 99-year mortgage were to hit the mainstream here in America, I hope that consumers will totally reject them.

I am disappointed to see that California has introduced the 50-year mortgage in order to cope with their ridiculous home prices.[1] Loaning more money to more people over longer periods is not the solution. In my opinion, this is akin to the government printing money. The easy availability of mortgage funds will artificially inflate California's housing market, causing the problem to escalate even further. An educated public will reject long-term mortgages for the betterment of their own finances and for a brighter future for the generation that follows.

## The Adjustable-Rate Mortgage (ARM)

If you use this product, you're playing with fire—and you will get burned! There is no better way to put it. Frankly, I have no idea why anyone would agree to a loan that might adjust to a higher interest rate. Adjustable-rate mortgages contributed in part to the burst of the housing bubble. Rates adjusted upwards just as the economy began to falter around 2007. Millions of Americans were left without jobs and no back-up money. When the interest rates adjusted upward, many homeowners saw their mortgage payments increase by 30-50%. Some individuals saw their house payments double. Most of these poor souls were already paying the outer limit of what they could afford for a home and had no room in their budget for expanding house payments. Mass foreclosures followed, with many Americans simply turning in their keys and walking away. As entire neighborhoods filled with boarded-up homes, real-estate values plummeted. As a result, many other homeowners who could actually afford their payments were thrust into negative equity overnight.

I'm sure many of these Americans were told, "If the rates go down, your house payment will be lower." That may have been enough to get many buyers to sign up. I'm sure those buyers left the deal with the sense that the banker was "looking out" for them. That he was "...helping them build a future and achieve their dreams." Call me a fuddy-duddy, I just don't trust banks. Perhaps my skepticism is due to my family's struggle during the Great Depression. My great-grandmother didn't trust anything a banker said. Heck, she buried her cash in jars. My point is, approach any mortgage dealings with attention and skepticism. If a banker tries to sell me on the idea that the interest rates may adjust down, I figure they could just as easily adjust up.

The adjustable-rate mortgage is a firecracker in a clenched hand. The fuse is burning and you're out of time. My best advice: Don't pick it up in the first place.

## The Home Equity Line of Credit (HELOC)

I know too many people who throw out the term HELOC as if they're some sort of financial savant. Here's a clue for all the financial gurus buying jet skis with their HELOC: IT'S A SECOND MORTGAGE! When I was a kid, I would always hear conversations about those neighbors or that distant cousin who had to take out a second mortgage. Usually, the story began with someone getting ill and having no money for hospital bills. Other stories involved failed businesses or ugly divorces. The term "second mortgage" always seemed to be tied to some sort of tragedy or deep personal problem. Granted, I was in grade school when I first remember being aware of these conversations, but I remember having a sense that second mortgages were not something you wanted to have. Even though I had little understanding of what a second mortgage was, I felt sorry for people who had to resort to one.

Consider the board game *Monopoly*. Mortgaging a property is something you do as a last resort, after you can no longer pay your bills. Players venture around the board paying cash for property, but they only resort to mortgages if they are in over their head. There is a reason for this. When *Monopoly* was developed in the 1930s, many people actually saved up and paid cash for their homes. At the same time, Henry Ford resisted the idea of offering financing for his automobiles. Between the *Monopoly* board and the whispers of second-mortgage hardships in my family, the word "mortgage" took on a negative connotation in my young mind.

It's obvious that big banking understood the public's negative association with the term "second mortgage." Otherwise, they wouldn't have renamed it "home equity line of credit." The game is the same; you take out a loan against the equity in your house. Only, the purpose of the HELOC is now different. Instead of using the HELOC as a last-ditch effort to ease the burden of a financial crisis, homeowners are using their equity to buy a bunch of depreciating assets like ATVs, RVs, boats, and motorcycles. I can almost understand those who use HELOCs to fund renovations. After all, the money is reinvested into the home. It's still better to renovate with cash. By contrast, taking your only appreciating material asset and tying up its value in depreciation is absolutely stupid! Homeowners are using these products to fund their toys because they don't have the cash on hand to purchase them outright. That's a sure indication that they can't afford those items in the first place.

The thing about HELOCs that aggravate me the most is the way they're marketed. One advertisement features a man fishing with his son in a new boat. The commercial makes an appeal to the viewer: "You can't afford *not* to spend this time with your children." The banks want you to feel that refusal to use their product is akin to failure as a parent. Worse yet, HELOC customers that I know generally boast about their new "financial freedom" to "accomplish their dreams"—as if their decision to take out a HELOC makes them feel financially superior.

There is nothing smart or superior about the home equity line of credit. It's just another way to separate a fool from his money.

### Reverse Mortgage

You have probably ascertained by now that I don't entirely trust banks. If there is one thing I distrust more than banks, its the financial products peddled on infomercials. Basically, any financial product sold on television should be avoided at all costs. I don't care which washed-out actor is vouching for it. One such reverse mortgage advertisement features a well-known celebrity claiming: "A reverse mortgage is not another way for them to take your house." If the first words in your commercial are an attempt to defend your product like that, it's probably safe to assume that it's a surefire way for them to take your house. Think about it. Some guy approaches you on the street asking for money. His first words to you are, "I'm a good person and you can trust me." He then goes on to explain why he's stuck in town with no money or identification and needing a bus ticket. A natural skeptic like myself thinks, "Since he has to loudly proclaim his goodness and trustworthiness, I shouldn't trust this guy." That's pretty much how I feel about these financial products advertised on television.

Another ad for reverse mortgages states the following: "Reverse mortgages are based on a notion that President Reagan signed into law..." Based on a *notion*? The last time I checked a civics textbook, presidents sign *laws* into effect, not *notions*. The fact that the ad made sure to mention Ronald Reagan makes me believe they are aiming to coerce older Americans into feeling that the reverse mortgage is safe and secure. The reverse-mortgage ads just smell untrustworthy.

Slimy ad campaigns are not my only reason for eschewing reverse mortgages. There are practical reasons as well. According to a 2017 article in *The Washington Post*, close to 90,000 reverse mortgage customers were in danger of losing their homes.[2] For those 90,000 poor souls, a reverse mortgage was, indeed, just another way for "them" to get your house. The article goes on to detail a half-dozen cases of elderly individuals, some widowed, who stand to lose their homes over small unpaid property taxes or outright deception by reverse-mortgage lenders.

Like most of my intended audience, you probably aren't of qualifying age for a reverse mortgage. However, you may have parents or other relatives who are. It's very important that you learn about the dangers of reverse mortgages and be prepared to spread that knowledge to your aging family members, lest they become taken in by one of their favorite 80's actors.

### Buy Flood Insurance (Even If "They" Say You Don't Need It)

Growing up in a flood-prone area of South Louisiana, the question of flood insurance was never really a question at all. I have witnessed several major flooding events during my 44 years, and I've seen underinsured homeowners lose everything time and time again. In 2016, a one-thousand-year rain event drenched the entire southern portion of our state, leaving a swamp of financial ruin in its wake. The worst victims were homeowners who did not have flood insurance simply because someone told them they were not in a flood zone. I wouldn't believe it if I hadn't seen it myself; real estate agents pushing sales forward by reminding prospective buyers that they won't have to deal with the expense of flood insurance. Always verify these claims.

Before purchasing our home in 2012, I made a trip to the Ascension Parish Drainage Board and located the most up-to-date flood maps I could find. What I discovered was that our agent was correct. Our prospective home was not in the flood zone. What she failed to mention was that the flood zone was only 50 yards from our property!

Additionally, the stated flood zone assumes that the Ascension Parish flood protection pumps are fully functional. One problem with the pumping station, and you might as well throw away the map. The first thing I did after signing the papers was buy flood insurance. Four years later when the catastrophic flood of 2016 crept within three feet of our home, my only worry was cleaning up the potential mess. I didn't have to fret about how to pay for it. Ultimately, the waters receded and left my home unharmed. So, did I feel it was worth it to renew my insurance? You bet I did!

Flood insurance offers one of the best bang-for-the-buck values in the insurance industry. If you are fortunate enough to live outside the flood plain, it's an even better value. I currently pay $486 per year for $200,000 of coverage. That's enough to tear the house down to the studs and replace everything inside. Basically, if you live anywhere besides a desert or mountain, flood insurance is a good idea.

# CORVETTE SUMMER

As a kid in the early 80s, I had two loves: *Star Wars* and Corvettes. The movie *Corvette Summer* (starring Luke Skywalker himself, Mark Hamill) had both. Hamill played a young man who rescued a yellow Corvette Stingray from the car crusher and spent his senior year in auto shop doing a full-out custom restoration. The 'vette is soon stolen, and hilarity ensues. The movie must have left an impression because I would one day attempt to rescue a yellow Stingray of my own—with equally laughable results. I went out to look at the car, and it was in dire straits. The car barely ran, the fiberglass had lost its gelcoat, and the interior was completely trashed. During the test drive, I knew in the pit of my stomach that it would be a terrible purchase. All concern subsided, however, when I mashed on the accelerator and felt the thrum of the 350 cubic-inch powerhouse stuffed up front.

Giving into my impulses (like I did with the Cavalier convertible), I forgot that there is a time and a place for performing a major car restoration. And that time is NOT when you are $10,000 in debt. The place is NOT under a one-slot open carport. Financing $3,500 for a 30-year-old car with major mechanical and cosmetic issues just screamed stupidity. (I wish Dave Ramsey had been there to scream it.) By the time I purchased the Corvette, I had spent my savings on a home renovation and had to resort to a three-year loan. With tax and interest included, I paid over $4,700 for a car that wouldn't stay running for more than a few minutes at a time. Including my car payment and student loans, I had racked up nearly $15,000 in debt.

Once again, my impulses led me to believe that I was "working so hard" and "really deserved it." Mark Hamill spent his *Corvette Summer* searching for his stolen 'vette. I spent mine hoping someone would steal it. Wouldn't have mattered; the damn thing would've stalled before the thief could've gotten away in it.

# 9

# TOYS, TRAVEL, AND HOBBIES

What would life really be if we didn't take some time to enjoy ourselves? When all else is said and done, we can't exist simply to work, sleep, and repeat. Even a hopeless tightwad like myself understands the need to have hobbies and interests. However, a balance must be struck between achieving our priorities while enjoying life. For me, the best way to enjoy life is to get the difficult parts over with so that I can focus on the fun. That is one of the many reasons I'm telling you to get out of debt as quickly as possible and get your financial priorities in order.

Once you are debt-free and have established your retirement and college savings, it is a good time to start enjoying your disposable income. I will not hesitate to inform you that this has been one of the most challenging arenas in my financial life. For most people (myself included), strict adherence to a budget and a strong sense of financial priorities will lead to fewer dollars available for fun stuff. Staying disciplined is difficult, especially when you look across the street and see your neighbors pulling out for their next offshore adventure in a $50,000 SUV with a $60,000 bay boat in tow. Even for me, it is sometimes difficult to remember that the vast majority of my neighbors and peers are in debt up to their eyeballs! That said, you can never really know for sure the finances of others.

Statistics tell us that most Americans are deep in debt and have little or no college or retirement savings. A 2018 report by the National Institute on Retirement Security indicates that nearly 60% of all Americans have no type of retirement savings account.[1] The statistics for college savings are nearly identical. Sallie Mae studied college savings among American families in 2016. Their finding? Nearly half of those polled indicated that they had not put aside money for their children's college education.[2] When I look at the lifestyles of my neighbors and peers, it's obvious to me that most of them are able to make payments on extravagant vehicles and toys because they're not saving enough for the future.

I love hobbies and I adore boats. I don't wish to dissuade you from enjoying your finances through boating, fishing, travelling, drag racing, model train building, or vacationing. My only wish is that each and every one of you achieve a state of financial order that allows you to *truly* afford to do these things without resorting to loans, second mortgages, or credit cards. I want you to enjoy your things knowing that you are not borrowing against your future (or that of your children). Will it be easy? Of course not! It takes planning, budgeting, saving, and discipline in order to attain these things without debt. Credit cards are easy. Second mortgages are easy. But then again, maybe that's why they are so bad for you financially.

Remember: Credit is a lie, whispering in your ear like the devil himself, promising that you can have all these things even though you don't have the money to pay for them. Assuming your financial house is in order, let's look at some of the common big-ticket leisure items you might be interested in.

### Boats

I would like to start with the big-ticket item that is at the top of my own list, the one material item I have yet to attain: a brand-new boat.

I currently own a small jon boat. It's an old hand-me-down from dad that I re-painted and continue to keep up. My reasons for waiting to purchase my dream boat are the same ones I will pass along to all of you. I am finally reaching a place financially that will allow me to make this dream come true—with careful planning and continued saving. You have probably heard the old adage that a boat is a hole in the water into which you toss your money. There is some truth to that. And that is exactly why boat ownership should only be attempted after you are debt-free. Like any major purchase, boats require a special set of considerations.

### A Tow Vehicle

The average boat owner will require a tow vehicle to move their boat from home to the launch. That single requirement really ups the ante for the price of getting on the water. If you don't already own a truck or SUV to pull your boat, you're about to experience the price creep that comes with boat ownership. The boat/tow vehicle question often creates a financial catch-22 that can be difficult to negotiate without careful planning. For example, you have your eyes on a boat that weighs about 3,000 pounds. You will need to upgrade to a truck or SUV to tow that boat. Unfortunately, you really have no other heavy-duty use for that vehicle. Keep in mind that most boat owners use their boats far less than they think they will. You must realize that you will be paying a stiff gas penalty all year long for the few week-ends you will actually be towing your boat. Many owners don't take this into consideration and ultimately end up with a boat payment, truck payment, higher insurance for both, and a large gasoline bill. I recommend buying your tow vehicle with cash one or two years before purchasing a cash boat.

I know more than a few people who refuse to go fishing unless they can gather three friends to split the gas bill. Their complaints usually sound something like this: "It costs me $200 every time I hitch up the boat." If you can't afford to use your own boat without splitting the cost, you can't afford the boat.

### Indoor Storage

If there is one thing I know about nice fiberglass boats, it's that THEY ROT! Any boat left out in the elements, even under a good quality cover, will quickly succumb to the elements. Yes, I know that many boats today feature wood-free "no-rot" construction. However, the vinyl upholstery and carpeting will turn to dust in a matter of a few years unless your boat is kept in covered storage. Simply put: If you can't afford to store your boat inside, you can't afford the boat.

A young woman I was dating during X-ray school accompanied me to a boat show once. My date and I were checking out a very nice cabin cruiser when she said to me, "If we get married, can we buy this boat? I don't care if we live in a trailer, as long as we have a boat like this." It was like hearing a giant needle scratch across a life-size vinyl record. By covered storage, I don't mean a pop-up carport in front of your mobile home. If you own a mobile home, you are losing thousands per year in depreciation. Parking an expensive, depreciating asset in the front of the depreciating asset you live in will only hurry your financial demise. Only after you are in your permanent home with either a shop or garage should you attempt to own a boat. It will last much longer (perhaps decades instead of years) if you are patient enough to purchase it when you are able to store it properly.

### Safety and Other Accessories

Another common mistake among first-time boat owners is failure to consider the cost of safety gear and other accessories. The most important piece of boat safety gear is your life jacket. Most of you are aware that water safety laws require life jackets for each passenger.

However, many states require additional equipment, such as fire extinguishers, sounding devices (horns or whistles), flares, and VHF radios, depending on the boat's size and intended use. Boats rarely come from the dealer or previous owner with all of these items. It's important to remember that all the aforementioned safety items must be properly stored and maintained in order to function if called upon. Even with impeccable maintenance, your fire extinguishers, life jackets, and flares have limited functional shelf life and must be replaced periodically. When purchasing a new boat, it is imperative that you plan for the cost of these items; they can easily add hundreds of dollars to your purchase.

If you are purchasing used, assess the condition of these items if they are included and be prepared to replace some of them if necessary. Having grown up on the water, I have seen many people killed in senseless boating accidents. Some of these deaths can be directly attributed to a lack of safety gear. Ironically, some accidents involve very expensive boats that are poorly maintained due to the owner's lack of funds. Remember, if you can't afford to properly maintain and stock your boat's safety gear, you can't afford the boat. Keep it simple and well within your budget and you are more likely to enjoy your purchase comfortably and safely.

### The Fish Didn't Get the Memo

My very first experience with marsh fishing was in April 2015. I had recently restored dad's old aluminum boat in lieu of buying a new fiberglass flats boat. While I was confident I could "afford the note" on that slick flats boat, I had recently decided that payments were just not my thing anymore. Besides, paying cash for my Honda Accord worked really well for me. Why not restore the old boat and pay cash for a new outboard? That way, I could have my boat and still be able to take vacations and do the other things I enjoyed using cash money. It was sort of like having my cake and eating it too!

With some guidance from my best friend and fishing buddy Leland, I started my first marsh trip with a bang. I pulled in a beautiful 27" redfish! Through the course of the day, we landed a dozen nice fish of several species. Grilling our catch the next afternoon, I thought to myself, "The fish didn't get the memo!" A fish doesn't care about the size of the boat on the other end of the line. I believe that many people overlook this simple fact in favor of justifying ridiculously expensive fishing boats. If you've ever known a hard-core bass fisherman, you've probably heard some of the many justifications for spending $60,000+ on a fishing boat. "You gotta get there fast so you can make more casts. The more casts you make, the more you up your chances of catching a fish." What if you had a slower boat but fished closer to the launch? You could make just as many casts. After all, the fish aren't confined to some place 10 miles upriver. I've seen this strategy work before. Strangely enough, a friend of mine once entered a local bass tournament. He won 1st prize by fishing at the boat launch while all the other contestants raced around the river for three hours!

The number one way to increase your fishing skills has nothing to do with your boat. Fancy electronics, expensive trolling motors, automatic stick anchors, and bass-fishing racing suits won't put more fish in the boat, either. Do you think that the fish care that your truck and boat have matching vinyl wraps? THEY DON'T! The best way to put more fish in the boat? Read books about fishing. Would it surprise you to know that my boat is equipped with zero electronics and an old-fashioned anchor? I am sporting about 230 fewer horsepower than the average bass boat, yet I succeed with most species I fish. I don't even own a single fishing rod that costs over $100. I improved my fishing by reading and practicing skills instead of relying on more "stuff."

### What Did That Fish Cost You?

I have devised a method of calculating the true cost of a boat and it works well for fishing boats, ski boats, and cruisers. Similar to the way in which we calculated a per-year cost for a car, we can calculate a per-use cost for a boat. According to Statista.com, bowriders, runabouts, and ski boats are used, on average, only 8 days per year![3] That means your first boating season in your $50,000 MasterCraft will cost you approximately $5,000 per outing (considering you manage to squeeze in 10 trips).

The truth is, most prospective boat owners believe they will boat every weekend and will have a constant supply of passengers with which to share the fun. I know from my own experience that life inevitably gets in the way. "Every weekend" soon dissipates to every other weekend and then down to once a month, if that. If we experience a particularly wet year here in South Louisiana, there may not be much of a boating season at all. Before making your purchase, consider whether you really want to eat the depreciation on something that will not be used very often. Consider whether you can afford to drive a gas guzzler all year long for those 8-12 days per year you will need it for towing. I'm not trying to talk you out of a boat; just be aware of your cost per use and let that data inform you as to the size and age of the boat you choose. As always I recommend putting in lots of research, buying used, and paying cash.

### RVs, ATVs, UTVs, and Bikes

Much like boats, the aforementioned items will suffer crushing depreciation once they arrive home; so it is important to buy used, pay cash, and only purchase these items if you have a place to store them. This is especially true for fifth wheels, trailers, and motorhomes. These rolling homes that look so sturdy are actually quite light and flimsy. Remember, travel trailers need to be light in order to be towed by a large variety of vehicles on the American road. Manufacture them too heavy, and it costs families much more money to enter the hobby. This, in turn, would hurt RV and travel trailer sales.

I don't intend to beat up on the RV industry. I'm sure that most of these products are well-built and carefully assembled. The fact remains, however, that most campers are framed up with light-weight wood. A crash will convert most of them into toothpicks. The wooden sub-frame, aside from being lightweight, will eventually rot if the camper is left out in the elements. If you don't believe me, peer into back yards as you travel around town. Campers left outside in the yard or driveway tend to look run-down, with mildew and mold often taking residence on the siding. RVs and campers under some type of permanent structure almost always look better and are sure to last longer. As is the case with boats, you cannot afford a camper, travel trailer, or RV that you can't afford to cover and maintain.

## Vacationing

Who doesn't love an epic vacation? My dad's hero was Clark W. Griswold of the *National Lampoon's Vacation* films. Although hijinks and disasters were never a part of our family vacations, my dad reflected the spirit of Chevy Chase's titular character in the way he wanted mom, sister, and I to enjoy summer. Summer vacations were an exciting event for us, especially since I could sense a change in dad's operating procedure while on every road trip. In contrast to the remainder of the year, our two-week vacations saw my father spend money. I could sense that the rules were different for the time we spent at hotels, restaurants, amusement parks, and the like. What I happened to be witnessing as a child was the one area where mom and dad really liked to spend money for enjoyment.

The days leading up to vacation were often filled with great learning experiences as well. Dad would wax the family car, explain the importance of careful vehicle maintenance, and review with us the itinerary and travel route. A day or two before departing, I would accompany dad to the bank where he would buy traveler's checks. For those of you who are not familiar with traveler's checks, allow me to explain. Before the advent of magnetic strips, credit cards were a hassle to use, and debit cards simply did not exist. Because cash could be stolen and was nearly impossible to replace on the road, banks would issue traveler's checks. Traveler's checks were usually purchased with cash and could be redeemed as cash. If the traveler's checks were stolen, their serial numbers could be phoned into a bank for quick and easy replacement. Traveler's checks were generally a safe, reliable method for carrying lots of cash on a vacation. Notice that I have used the word "cash" an awful lot in the last few sentences.

In a society of instant gratification, it is so easy to swipe a credit card in order to make your dream vacation a reality. (I'm sure there are many folks out there who reserve their vacations on a credit card and immediately log into their account and pay the balance in full from a debit card. My guess is that those folks are few and far between). In fact, most people I've talked to will put a $5,000 Disney vacation on a credit card six weeks out and spend the next six months trying to pay back the vacation. In many of those cases, a medical emergency or car repair pops up, adding to the balance and postponing payoff for a year or more.

My dad had a particular saying when it came to vacations and credit cards: "There is no sense in paying for a vacation after it's already over!" I've heard him say it many times, and it stuck so well that I've always had my vacations paid in full long before they begin. Like anything else, the sacrifices involved with planning and saving for vacation are considerable, but the rewards are immeasurable.

### Start a Vacation Envelope

Michele and I celebrate the beginning of each one of our vacations at least 18 months in advance. We have a ritual that usually takes place within days of returning from our prior vacation. We pull out a plain paper envelope and mark it with some sort of symbol representative of our next big trip. We have adorned envelopes with Mickey ears for Disney trips, pictures of beach umbrellas for coastal getaways, even pictures of mountains for our ski trips. We then settle on an amount with which to stuff the envelope every time we receive a paycheck. Typically, we place a crisp $100 bill in the envelope each pay period for a savings of $300-$400 per month. After 12 months, we typically amass about $3,600. That's usually enough to reserve our vacation. The remaining months see us continuing to stuff the envelope for our spending money. While we stuff the vacation envelope, we place all of our loose change in a jar dedicated for snacks and meals on the road. During a typical savings cycle, we usually build up about $100 in pocket change for our trip.

The week leading up to our trip is when things get *really* technical. We gather up several additional envelopes and create an envelope budget system for our entire vacation. Using our budgeted route and vehicle's gas mileage as a guide, we estimate our fuel costs and place the appropriate amount of money in an envelope. We even draw a picture of a gas gauge on the front of the envelope (the gauge reads full, of course). Fun with envelopes doesn't stop there. We have an envelope for groceries (usually with a picture of a grocery cart on front) and an envelope containing money to spend at our favorite Irish pub when passing through Pensacola (that one gets a four-leaf clover). No matter how you decide to adorn your vacation envelopes, the important thing is that you budget for every type of spending you may encounter in the same manner you would your everyday household budget.

### Budgeting for Uncertain Costs

If you are unsure about the exact costs of some of your vacation budget items, congratulations! That means you are putting a lot of thought into your trip. Many vacationers underestimate some of their costs simply because they don't think down the road (pun intended). One good example of this is fuel costs. Early in my vacationing career, I estimated fuel costs based on the price of fuel at home. I should have considered increased costs along the highway or at my destination. In those cases, I found myself pulling out the debit card.

Believe it or not, I've attempted to predict where I might stop for gas and checked prices in those areas. That method proved to be quite tedious and time consuming. Instead, estimate your fuel consumption based on your vehicle's mileage and the travel distance plus 10%. I find that usually puts me right where I need to be in terms of gas money. You can do a similar calculation for groceries and dining. Adding 10% to your estimate will usually cover any fluctuating costs in that arena as well. And when planning your dining budget, don't forget to include tips!

# MY SHIRT WAS PLAID (WITH A BUTTERFLY COLLAR)

Spring, 1989. I tried to maintain my composure in spite of the snickering that filled the room. I knew going in that I was likely to face fierce ridicule, but I made this compromise with mom in an attempt to minimize the social damage. Mom volunteered at the church fellowship center taking in donations and re-distributing them to underprivileged families. When my sister and I were children, mom would often bring home broken down or abandoned toys that were fit for the junk pile. I would often cannibalize them for motors and wires or fix them if possible. That was all fun until the seventh grade, when mom started bringing home old clothing.

She once heard the rap song *Parents Just Don't Understand* by D.J. Jazzy Jeff and the Fresh Prince (The Fresh Prince, as in Will Smith). She must have misunderstood the line in the song in which Will Smith laments about receiving a plaid shirt with a butterfly collar. Soon after the song was a hit, I received a vintage 70's-era, plaid butterfly-collared shirt fresh from the donation desk. My flat refusal to wear the shirt to school led to some heated debates with my parents. In an attempt to placate mom while containing the damage to my social life, I agreed to wear it to Sunday school instead. I would receive two hours of sharp-tongued ridicule I would never forget. Will Smith was right after all; parents just don't understand.

It was around this time that I began to see that our family was doing things a little bit differently. At first, the word "budget" began to take on a negative connotation. As far as I knew, "the budget" was the reason I wouldn't be joining my peers in the designer jeans section of the department store. Looking back on it now, it's definitely for the best. (Google: "Z. Cavaricci blue jean pant suit" and I'm sure you'll agree.) Being the kid at school with Walmart jeans and a 12-year-old beater was hard at times, but it taught me valuable life lessons. I learned early on to put my needs first, then work and save for my wants. When I finally saved up enough money for some name-brand clothes, I didn't want to spend it easily. I bought a few nice pieces, saved them for Fridays, and took great care of them. Tinkering on the Pinto, I developed in-depth automotive skills; all of which I still use to save money today!

# 10

# BUDGET BUSTERS

It's true, me and "the budget" started out on difficult terms. Eventually, I came to understand the freedom that a carefully planned budget provides. Still, there are countless distractions that seek to grab our attention and move our behavior toward actions that invite financial chaos. This chapter will discuss some of the cultural constructs that threaten to derail our resolve and move us toward a life of financial servitude.

## Beware the Entitlement Trap

Many new graduates (myself included) have been distracted by the entitlement trap. We complete college with the idea that we should have the same lifestyle as our parents the very same day we graduate. After all, we just suffered through four years of classes, projects, exams, and stress. We deserve a new car and a house in a gated community, right? Our feelings of entitlement are often compounded by a culture obsessed with instant gratification. As a result, we fail to consider the many years of toil and sacrifice our parents endured to reach their goals and attempt to reproduce or exceed the lifestyle we experienced while growing up. We all know at least one person or couple caught in this trap.

College graduation is followed immediately by marriage, two new cars, and a brand-new home—all within a year or two. It's all fun and exciting for the young happy couple until the student-loan papers start reaching the new address. Our couple is caught in an ever-escalating cycle of debt-creep as the many expenses they failed to consider begin to pile up, and they are forced to charge their groceries on credit cards. I've been there. I have friends who have been there and friends who are headed that way.

### The Nature of "Affordability"

American society wants us to believe we can "afford" anything we are able to finance. In today's modern age, that includes just about anything. I recently brought my mountain bike in for service and could not help but notice a large poster on the storefront window stating: "Ask about our convenient financing." Are you kidding? Finance a bicycle! A more common example is jewelry. If you were to consider purchasing a $5,000 engagement ring but only had $1,000, I would tell you that you can't afford it. The jeweler, on the other hand, will smile and assure you that you can afford the piece on his ultra-convenient finance plan.

Since when did we decide to allow salesmen to dictate to us what we can and can't afford? After all, the jeweler doesn't work my job for me. He doesn't pay my utilities or contribute to my 401(k). How does he know what I can and can't afford? The jeweler, the car salesman, the appliance guy, and many other vendors are simply trying to prevent you from looking at the big picture. Monthly payments keep you hemmed into living paycheck to paycheck. Once you have expended your monthly income on "convenient payments," you are unable to make plans past the next set of payments due. We typically think of the phrase "living paycheck to paycheck" as applying to the working poor. In reality, living paycheck to paycheck is the lifestyle of most middle-class Americans.

Financing, credit, car leases, and convenient payments sound somewhat different, but they all represent the same lie. Financing is a lie! It's a lie that attempts to convince you that whatever you want can be yours, even if you have no money. We often rationalize our decision to believe this lie through a process I call *financial relativism*. We make errant decisions about what we can afford based on what our peers are purchasing. You may have caught yourself at some point checking out a neighbor or co-worker's new truck thinking, "I make about what he makes, so if he can afford it, I can too." Like convenient payments, financial relativism works to keep our focus away from the big picture. If we were to apply a big-picture approach to our peer's apparent successes, we might second-guess whether that person is saving enough for retirement or their children's college fund. The fact is, we only see what our peers want us to see. We see the new Mercedes SUV across the street, but we aren't privy to the owner's retirement account—or credit card bill. We hear the rumble of the four-wheel-drive next door pulling in with the bass boat, but we don't hear that couples' money fights.

The truth about affordability is this: If you don't have the cash on hand to buy it, you can't afford it! The cash-only lifestyle works, and not just among the ultra-rich. It works for me and it will work for you, too. When you commit to only paying cash, you will walk away from every purchase with pride and confidence knowing that you own that item. You really *own* it. And you will never have to lose a single night of sleep wondering if you can really afford it!

## Confusion About "Wants" and "Needs"

There is no force of nature that is capable of wrecking your household finances more effectively than confusion over wants and needs.

Our society uses the word "need" so carelessly that it has essentially lost its meaning. My father instilled in me a unique philosophy concerning needs, one that was no doubt honed by his parents who had suffered through the Great Depression as children. For my grandparents, Christmas was not a time for receiving piles of toys and goodies. Instead, the simple pleasure of making homemade candy meant a season well-celebrated. Although my father grew up in considerably better circumstances, he never lost touch with where his family came from. He honored the struggle they endured so that he could grow in faith and knowledge to become our family's first college graduate.

Compared to my father and his parents before him, my sister and I were spoiled through and through. Like many in our generation, we began to strip the word "need" of any practical meaning. My first lesson on wants vs. needs came from my dad. I think I was in "need" of a $75.00 pair of designer jeans (Z. Cavaricci's, I'm embarrassed to say). Of course, I "needed" them in order to fit in with the cool kids. Dad would say, quite matter-of-factly, "Son, your only needs in this world are food, water, and shelter." Actually, that made sense. In Boy Scouts, the first thing we learned about camping was to secure a shelter, get access to clean water, and then concern ourselves with food. Food, water, and shelter are the three reasons we toil at work every day. All needs should factor down to one of these. If not, you are dealing with a want. It's as simple as that. Even by my very strict definition of a need, there is still some amount of wiggle room. For example, a mansion is a shelter, yet it does not exactly qualify as a need. Likewise, a $300 steak dinner is food, but you don't "need" it.

Which brings me to my next point: luxuries as needs. Think about how many single people out there are driving massive 7-seater SUVs with 10,000-pound towing capacities but don't have a family to pack in them or a horse trailer to pull. I've heard them say, "I need the off-road capability." Why? Are you driving across the Sahara? Here's a hint: Off-road capability does not factor down into food, water, or shelter. Of course, for someone who has all of their financial priorities in check, I say, "Go out and get that big SUV—used—with cash.

Having restored a small boat for recreation and fishing, I spend time on boating-related forums. You might be surprised by what people will pass off as needs when it concerns recreation time. "I need to upgrade to a V8 boat in order to water ski." Really? Because I learned how to ski behind a 14ft. jon boat with a 20-horsepower outboard—and there were three adults, a gas tank, and an ice chest in the boat slowing it down. Boats are not a need, skiing is not a need, and V8 boats are certainly not a need. However, they are all really cool *wants* that are great to have as long as your other priorities are in check.

### Socially-Imposed "Needs"

In the context of our modern society, many conveniences have reached need status. Cellular phones are a perfect example of this. Our grandparents didn't have to carry a cellular phone or worry about providing one for each family member over six years old. One phone per household was plenty enough, and it was permanently attached to the wall. I would argue that my grandfather's phone bill represented a much smaller percentage of his income than the cellular phone bill does in relation to the modern family budget. Another example of this phenomenon is cable. In just one decade, most families went from free television to some form of fee-for-service entertainment, like cable or satellite. Again, employers didn't just raise everyone's pay in order to help provide their employees with these new needs. These items simply cut deeper into the household budget.

While cable or satellite can never come close to qualifying as a need, I admit that it has become very difficult to work efficiently without a cellular phone in our society. Cellular phones have become so difficult to live without, they tend to feel like needs. In spite of this, cellular phones should never be allowed to wreck your family finances. The bottom line: Buy the least expensive phone available and roll with it until your debts are paid and your retirement and college accounts are set up. If you have money left over after that, continue to hold off until your job responsibilities absolutely demand the features a fully-optioned phone has to offer. Otherwise, it's just a toy.

I have only just upgraded from a flip phone to a smartphone within the last few months. My reason for holding out? I felt like the text and photo functions of my flip were adequate for dealing with my everyday work requirements. As my responsibilities grew, I found it more and more inconvenient to text multiple employees while writing the schedule or dealing with emergencies. All the while, I had been saving money for a big upgrade... for my wife. She received a new smartphone and I took her old one. I estimate that my reluctance to upgrade phones saved me upwards of $10,000 over the past 15 years. I spent most of my cellular-phone years paying only $30 per month for service.

As for cable/satellite, I only had cable for 8 years of my adult life. It doesn't take long for most cable subscribers to realize they are paying for many more channels than they actually enjoy. Of course, this has resulted in millions of families already cutting cable in favor of internet-based programming. Switching to a streaming service can save significant money; however, subscribing to several at a time can be costlier than cable. Cable is a luxury that we can live without. Quite honestly, most people would be better off without it. Since I cut cable for good (about 10 months ago), I've read countless books, earned an additional professional license, restored an antique tractor, and written almost half of this book! The savings alone (about $100 per month) paid for the beach vacation I am currently enjoying while typing this very sentence.

∽

### What the Naysayers Say (and What They Actually Mean)

Several times throughout the course of this book, I have mentioned the "naysayers." In fact, I have found myself quoting them so often that I've decided to devote a small part of this chapter to their ignorance. We all know someone who plays Debbie Downer to any idea we have. So much so, we begin to avoid sharing our plans with this individual (or individuals). Financial naysayers are particularly annoying to me, and it's because I have made mistakes in the past based on their poor arguments and peer pressure. Luckily, years of life experience and financial stability has taught me how to critique their questionable advice and negative banter. A recent interaction with one of my peers perfectly illustrates the concept of the financial naysayer.

Michele and I dream of one day owning a nice powerboat. Each March, we attend the local boat and RV show that is held at an expo center just a few miles up the road. After seeing our fill of powerboats, fishing lures, and outdoor products, we decided to take an unusual detour into the RV section. We've always agreed that an RV or travel trailer was not really worth sinking money into. They are built flimsily, they need to be stored under some type of structure, and they depreciate worse than cars and boats. However, our interior design backgrounds called us to look over what's new in the world of RV and travel trailer interiors. After touring a couple of models, we walked out with some good ideas for hidden storage and space-savings that we thought we might apply to our own home. Michele expressed an interest in camping, but we both agreed that an RV or travel trailer was not an expense in which we wanted to partake. I suggested to Michele that we try tent camping, something we had wanted to try for several years. As new empty-nesters, we now had time to explore tent camping together for the first time.

Back at work on Monday, the subject of the boat and RV show came up almost immediately. Expecting my peers to react with some level of positive input, I excitedly shared my plans to take Michele tent camping. Instead, my plans were met with blank stares and sarcasm. "Your tent will leak." "Your wife will hate sleeping on the ground." "There's no bathroom out there." "Mosquitoes." Those were just a few of the responses. Then came exactly what I expected to hear: "You need a camper!" "I would never go out to the woods without a camper!" "We bought a camper last year and they worked with us and got the payments right where we could afford it!" "I know a guy and he can put you in a toy hauler for only $150/mo."

Where was the openness to my deciding to rough it? I'm an Eagle Scout, after all. I can light a fire without matches. I can boil eggs in a paper bag and build campfire seats out of limbs and vines. And that's a heck-of-a lot cheaper than picking up a 15-year note on a camper. "You'll see!" they teased, "Michele will hate it out there and she will either refuse to go back without a camper or she might never want to go back at all. If you enjoy camping, you best go out and get a camper first!" At first, I came away with the impression that my friends really enjoy their campers and that they were genuinely concerned with whether or not my wife would enjoy her first outdoor stay. A few weeks of thought and one very successful tent-camping weekend later, I began to reconsider what they were *really* trying to say.

### Naysayers Aren't Concerned with Your Happiness

Don't believe for one minute that the Negative Nellies and Debbie Downers of your world are attempting to steer you away from a bad experience. The point they are attempting to get across has nothing to do with you. It is the naysayers who are miserable, and they want you to join them in their struggle! When someone tells you that you have to own an RV to have fun in the woods, what they are actually saying is that they are up to their eyeballs in debt and want you to join them in their misery. When your coworker says, "You can stretch those payments out for a long time to make it affordable," he is really saying, "I will be upside-down on this RV for the next 12 years, and I would like a friend who understands my pain." At the end of the day, your coworkers and neighbors who are in massive debt know that they are in financial trouble. The only remedy in sight? Pull everyone else into the same hole so they don't have to feel alone.

### Naysayers Are Jealous of Your Contentment

The naysayer is attempting to turn the tables on you. He or she wants the happiness and contentment that you show when you are living a debt-free lifestyle. When a peer says to me, "Your wife will hate tent camping and never want to go with you again!," what that person is really saying is, "I wish my wife enjoyed tent camping. Instead, I had to go $40,000 in debt to get her to try the state park." When I hear, "I like the convenience of having a kitchen and bathroom," what I actually hear is, "I don't have the skill to cook outdoors or dig a latrine." Besides, if you love the convenience of plumbing and a full kitchen, why go camping anyhow? Or my personal favorite: "You can't attach a toy-hauler to a tent." In which case, I hear: "I'm too lazy to walk from the campsite to the pool, so I'm also in debt $10,000 for a four-wheel-drive golf cart." The fact is, the naysayers lack your contentment! Your very ability to avoid debt by making do with less is enviable to them. Unfortunately, naysayers are naysayers simply because they don't want to admit they are jealous of your happiness.

### Naysayers Are Normalizing Debt in Our Society

The aforementioned situations don't strictly apply to RVs. Naysayers entangle themselves in any conversation involving debt for just about any consumer product. They know all too well they got a terrible deal on that truck, boat, RV, etc. Instead of attacking the problem, they attempt to convince more people to take on the same debt. When most of their peers are in the same situation, a normalization effect occurs. Your friends, co-workers, and neighbors begin to view massive debt as a normal part of everyday suburban life. After all, when everyone on the block is doing it, it can't be wrong? Right? This concept is very similar to the old cliché about "keeping up with the Jones's." The Jones's buy a new car, then you feel you have to have a new car as well, then your other neighbor, and so on and so forth. They seek to recruit more individuals into a bottomless pit of debt by extolling the virtues of the many great things they own (while, of course, leaving out the part about having to buy groceries on a credit card last month because junior needed school uniforms). Beware of the rhetoric of the naysayer, he or she is attempting to pull you in. In fact, be proud of the fact that you are the naysayer's target (it probably means you are doing something right).

# THE HEART ATTACK

September, 1998. My family was returning from vacation in Gulf Shores, Alabama when dad grew quiet. He had complained of a nagging pain between his shoulder blades that started as we left the condo for home. He had asked mom to drive after filling up the car a few minutes earlier; this was most unusual. He leaned in closer to mom and asked her to take him to Baldwin County Hospital a few minutes up the road. Dad never complained, so I knew something was desperately wrong. I sat helplessly in the rear passenger-side seat trembling, wringing my hands and shaking my right leg as I do when I feel agitated. All I could see of my dad was his left arm, slowly turning ever-more sickly shades of green.

Outside the hospital, I paced nervously while attempting to contact family. I thought of the 15 years of careful diet combined with all the attention to exercise and fitness. Was it all for naught? I mean, dad lived eight years longer than my grandfather before suffering his heart attack. Did dad's rock-solid discipline really help the situation? Should he have just blown his money and had fun? Should he have eaten whatever he wanted and not worried about the daily walks? At the time, I was three months away from graduating college. Would dad live to see it? I remember at that moment feeling a deep temptation to abandon discipline and adopt a "seize the day" mentality. I suddenly realized that I faced the same fundamental question that my father faced when my grandfather passed. Dad, too, was in college when my grandfather died—nearly 30 years to the day.

There is, however, one monumental difference in the two situations. My dad just celebrated his seventieth birthday. Not only did he survive his heart attack and the quadruple bypass that followed, but he flourished. Dad attended every cardiac rehab appointment and returned to his routines with even more determination. He exercised harder, ate healthier, and continued with a discipline that his doctors have described as legendary. I firmly believe dad's determination to thwart his family's health history put him in the physical condition necessary to survive the first few minutes of that heart attack because it bought him the time necessary to get appropriate care.

The legacy of that event lives on in the decisions I make every day. Do I seize the day or plan for the future? Should I believe in the consequences of lifestyle or leave it up to fate? When it came down to lifestyle and fitness, I made the decision long ago to make healthy eating and exercise a top priority. Where I struggled was finances. The temptation for me to "seize the day" is palpable... albeit for good reason. What I've learned over the years is that fitness and finances can complement each other in surprising ways! In the chapter ahead, I'll show you how.

# 11

# FINANCE AND FITNESS

You've probably heard the phrase "Cleanliness is next to Godliness." I subscribe closely to that theory. In fact, I add to the idea three considerations:

1. *Cleanliness is next to a balanced checkbook.*

2. *A balanced checkbook is next to financial stability.*

3. *Financial stability is next to physical fitness.*

Sound like a stretch? Allow me to elaborate. In my experience, a messy home is a sure sign that the homeowner's checkbook is in shambles. After all, a person who can't pick up after themselves probably isn't taking the time to check the bank balance. Sound judgmental? It is, but you've stuck with me this far, so I hope you'll forgive me. And yes, I still balance my checkbook every day with the old-fashioned checkbook ledger. For those of you keeping your checkbooks balanced, you are probably also enjoying some level of financial success. What matters is that you are paying attention to your money. You know exactly where you stand and that is absolutely necessary to make plans for where you want to go. Cleanliness, in the context of money management, is the first step towards meeting your goals. Yet, there remains an additional benefit to competent money management: physical fitness.

## The Financially Fit Have More Free Time

Just imagine if you had enough money to meet your obligations plus some to put away for the future. Chances are, you wouldn't feel forced to work extra jobs. Living a cash-only lifestyle means that you don't owe anyone anything. You don't have to take that part-time job to help pay off the truck. You don't need a side hustle to get the electrical problems repaired on your camper. Is a side hustle a bad thing? Of course not. However, it's much more fun when you *want* to perform your side hustle than when you *need* to perform your side hustle. The less expenses you burden yourself with, the less you have to work to keep up with them. That directly equates to more time for leisure and exercise. That, in turn, will bring less stress and better physical and mental health.

## Golf Cart Crazy

I don't know about you, but when I look around the neighborhood, I feel as though everyone has gone golf cart crazy! Want to go fish the neighborhood pond? Hop in the golf cart! Need to stop by the Henderson's three doors down? "Honey, fire up the golf cart!" The mailbox is a staggering 50 feet from the front door. Better back down the driveway in the golf cart! And I'm not talking about your generic, run-of-the mill, white golf cart either—that might make financial sense! No, what we have here are jacked-up, chromed-out, four-wheel-drive, hi-fi stereo, flames on the door, six-passenger, stretched-out, widened-up, KC-Daylighted, K&N filtered, glass-packed, turbo-charged, not-allowed-on-any-golf-course-whatsoever... golf cart. It's no wonder Americans are so broke, and so overweight. Is there anyone out there that really and truly *needs* a golf cart to ride through the subdivision, or to go to the mailbox? I've overheard the guy one street over mention that he has over $15,000 invested in his custom cart alone. That's not counting the toy hauler it fits in and the truck to tow it all. He "needed" something for his kids to drive to the pool while they are "camping" in the mansion-on-wheels that he keeps parked in the backyard. Is it any surprise to you that this particular neighbor and his children are obese?

When a normal, middle-class family commits itself to a cash-only lifestyle with priorities in check, there won't be thousands of dollars lying around waiting to be wasted on custom golf carts (or most other wheeled toys, for that matter). Sticking to a financial plan means that family will not acquiesce to swiping a credit card to attain that toy either. The result: A healthy family whose kids walk down to the pond, walk to the neighbors, and run or bike if they want to get anywhere fast. Will your kids hate you? No, but they might say they do. When I was a kid, I thought I hated my dad because he refused to buy me a Go Kart. He held his ground and, as a result, I've remained a healthy weight throughout my life. Dad prevented me from developing the habit of hopping on an ATV anytime I wanted to go farther than 50 feet. Now, I prefer to walk whenever possible.

If you resist the temptation to go golf cart crazy, you will naturally get more exercise. Your family will do the same. You will save cash, taxes, and interest by avoiding the purchase. Fewer toys also means less time at work and less time spent maintaining toys. You will free up money and time for more important, permanent things, such as savings and family time. As a result, you will ultimately be healthier both physically and financially!

## Behold the Power of the Sandwich

Did you know that the single greatest weapon in the war of fitness and finance is the humble sandwich? Right about the time I took my first job, I read an article claiming that brown-bagging your lunch could save you up to $1,200 per year. Naturally, I tested the idea by bringing a sandwich to work every day instead of going out or ordering in for lunch. It's hard to say if I actually saved $1,200 because I didn't spend a year ordering lunch before that. I do know, however, that my grocery bill ran about $70-$100 per month. That was pretty low even for 1999 standards. Additional reinforcement came from the constant complaints of my coworkers who lamented the fact that they could never get their credit cards paid off due to all of their lunch charges. Oddly enough, they were the same coworkers who teased me incessantly about eating fat-free bologna on white while they gorged themselves on Applebee's. I never took it personally. Instead, I realize that they were inviting me to join them in the broke and out-of-shape club. I resisted, and my retirement savings grew while my beltline shrank.

Preparing your own lunch is one of the best ways you can improve your financial and physical fitness. By the way, I define "prepare your own lunch" as shopping for staple items and then assembling those items into salads, wraps, sandwiches, etc. TV dinners don't count. "Fat free" TV dinners don't count, either. When you purchase TV dinners, you are purchasing a high-sodium (even if not a high-fat) meal that you are paying someone else to prepare. You are also paying for the package and that little throwaway microwave tray. TV dinners will defeat the entire purpose of this section, so please, avoid them at all cost. Salads, wraps, sandwiches, etc. cost less to purchase and assemble. Generally, these items offer lower fat, sodium, and empty calories than TV dinners. Something as simple as tuna, crackers, an energy bar, and a water can make up a cheap and healthy portable lunch. I lived off that very diet during three years of

X-ray and radiation therapy school. There, too, I gleefully accepted the ridicule of my peers.

Starting on Monday, make a commitment to prepare your lunch every day for the next three months. Additionally, make a concerted effort to put away the money you save instead of spending it on something else. You might be surprised by how much extra cash you are able to gather!

## Good Habits Carry Over

As you can see, it's no accident that those who are financially responsible tend to also be responsible with their health and well-being. Many attributes are shared between the wealthy and the healthy. Most wealthy people achieve their wealth by setting goals, measuring their progress, and paying attention to the results. If you would like to retire a millionaire, for instance, you would first have to set the goal of "I want to retire with one million dollars in the bank." You would next draw up a plan outlining how much you would need to save each year to meet that goal. As years go by, you would measure your progress through net-growth calculations and adjust where necessary. This is the same mindset applied by any person who is attempting to meet a fitness goal. Once you master the skill of planning and goal-setting for either finance or fitness, the other will occur more naturally to you. It's just a matter of getting started.

## Health and Wealth in My Own Life

Watching someone you love suffer through an illness can have a profound effect on your future. Dad's heart attack at age 50 was a wake-up call for me. Dad took pretty good care of himself. Everyone in our family knew his risk factors. Perhaps we thought his exercise and diet would prevent him from having to deal with his family history of heart disease. Soon after he fell ill, I questioned whether or not I should even bother with a healthy lifestyle. Should I not bother saving and just live for the day? Those questions weighed on me heavily for several days. As the mental fog cleared, I came to the realization that my dad, unlike his father, survived his heart attack. This was probably due to the fact that dad made exercise an integral part of his life. Dad had been prescribed cholesterol meds and an exercise regimen 15 years earlier. Dad's commitment to exercise for those 15 years may have been the one factor that added up to him coming home from the hospital. I decided then and there, at 22 years of age, that I was not going to cave into the fear of what might be. I was going to face my family history the best way I knew how. I committed to make exercise and a healthy diet a top priority in my life.

Believe it or not, many people have called my reasoning into question. Many have asked, "What happens if you die anyway? Won't you wish you had enjoyed that money instead of hoarding it all those years?" Quite frankly, I *will* die anyway. Eventually. If I die before enjoying my retirement, my last thought won't be, "I wish I'd had a bigger boat." It'll be, "I'm glad I have that money put away so my wife doesn't have to struggle." It's true, you can't take it with you. Sometimes, being a man means leaving something behind as opposed to making sure nothing is left.

Deciding at a young age to adjust my diet has had many fringe benefits. I've already mentioned how preparing your own meals can save thousands of dollars per year. I originally learned how to prepare my own meals in order to keep the fat and sodium content under control. Saving money was a secondary benefit in that particular case. Meal planning, in turn, necessitated careful planning of my budget and schedule, which led me to develop habits and routines that I utilize to this day. For me, health and wealth have been married since my first days as a bachelor. Because of that, I believe effort aimed at improving one will always positively improve the other.

Like every good habit, the path to financial and physical fitness is not easily negotiated. My grandfather's untimely death and my father's quadruple bypass have been powerful motivating factors for me. When I walk, jog, hike, pedal, or paddle, I am just as much fighting for my life as I am simply enjoying exercise. That fight is at the forefront of my mind every time I take on physical activity. In the case of finances, my desire to leave a legacy for my family is as important as my quest to retire comfortably. I realize I may not, in spite of my best efforts, finish the race. Rest assured, my family will.

When the simple act of exercise became "fighting for my life," some interesting things started to happen. I began to see unhealthy foods and activities very differently. Fast food began to look like poison... literally. Every time I stopped for fast food or fried foods, I could only think of the fat globules floating through my bloodstream searching out a deadly spot to roost in my arteries. It wasn't long before I looked at fast food as a form of slow-acting poison. For someone who ate fast food three to four times a week as a college student, that revelation was life-changing. To this day, I rarely stop at a fast food chain more than once or twice a year—and only under extreme circumstances. Meanwhile, on the finance side, I began to see debt as a slow-acting poison as well, sabotaging my plans for financial growth.

### Credit Cards Are Cookies; Debt Is Trans-Fat

At 23 years of age, I was looking at fast food vendors as poison peddlers. Cookies and cake, however, was an entirely different story. I have never met a carbohydrate that I didn't like! And I love dipping my cookies and cakes (and most other carbs) in milk. For me, to see a cookie is equal to eating a cookie. Like cookies and cake, credit cards can be a nearly impossible habit to break. Credit cards are now an integral part of American culture; they are as ubiquitous to our modern lives as six-shooters to the Old West cowboy. Fortunately, the solution to my dependence on credit cards was as simple as that of cookies and cake. Don't keep them in the house! If I buy a bag of cookies or bake a cake, I will eat all of it in a matter of two sittings. I stopped buying both many years ago. I just don't keep them in the house. The same goes for credit cards. It's best if you don't bring them home in the first place. If they have taken up residence in your wallet, cut them up.

Remember a few years back when the federal government began requiring food manufacturers to include trans-fat content on all of their labeling? The backlash against trans-fat was so severe that its use was banned in many municipalities across the country. What is trans-fat, anyway? Simply put, trans-fat is a type of fat created in a lab by food companies. Its purpose is to imitate the good qualities of real fats (flavor, moistness, mouth-feel) while reducing the negative effects, such as limited shelf life. Unfortunately, it was discovered that trans-fats were not metabolized by the human body the same way as their all-natural brethren. Trans-fats have, subsequently, been linked to the rise of heart disease in modern society. Truth be told, trans-fat is probably more akin to plastic than food. Remember when I mentioned that I love dipping my carbs in milk? I used to crush cookies in a bowl of milk quite often. I quit doing that rather abruptly one day after stirring my "cookie soup" with a plastic spoon. The spoon came out of the bowl with this pasty coating... the fat? I thought, "The fat in these cookies is attracted to plastic... that can't be healthy." I quit bringing cookies home after that.

Debt is a lot like trans-fat. It is a lie that masquerades as something it's not. I've said it before, but it bears repeating. Debt promises that you are wealthy and deserving. It deceives you into believing that any lifestyle is yours. It claims to be the great equalizer that puts you on par with the well-to-do folks that you admire so much. Don't be fooled. Like pasty plastic-fat stuck to a spoon, debt accumulates on top of itself. It multiplies until it plugs your finances and constricts your very heart. The best solution to debt? It's no different than cookies, cakes, credit cards, and trans-fats—just don't bring it home!

## 12

---

# SIMPLICITY

The casual bystander in the 1990s would never have suspected my father earned a six-figure salary. He wore Rustler blue jeans, button-down shirts from Walmart, and drove a brown compact car. Simplicity came easy for him because it was all he knew as a boy. Dad's grandparents were farmers. They survived the Great Depression on cash crops, logging, odd jobs, even frog hunting. My great grandfather's family lived in a proverbial two-room shack. The two halves of their house were separated by a large curtain with the rear half serving as the sleeping quarters and the front half as the kitchen. The kitchen was complete with indoor plumbing via a sink with an old-fashioned hand pump. All other plumbing was handled out back. Life might have been a struggle for my great-grandparents, but they were happy people who understood the value of a dollar. My dad spent much of his childhood helping on their farm and it no doubt shaped his ideas about money, life, and happiness. To this day, he prefers the simplicity of gardening over the many complex and expensive hobbies he could easily afford.

The comedian Jeff Foxworthy remarked during a stand-up routine: "Men are very simple. We want a beer and we want to see something naked." I sometimes wish that were really true (of myself, anyway). The truth is, we are all somewhat complex. We are searching, confused, self-contradicting, imperfect creatures who are, for the most part, constantly striving. Our striving, whether it be for knowledge or material gain, can leave us feeling physically and mentally cluttered. We bombard ourselves with stuff. The world bombards us with seemingly endless media: news, television, music, gaming, pop culture. In our society of mass consumption and instant media, there often seems to be no escape. No peace. In order to achieve the ideal set forth in this book, it helps to adopt an attitude of simplicity. Don't panic, I'm not talking about monastery life. Rather, I suggest paring down, ridding yourself of the noise and clutter.

### Less is More

I was first introduced to the phrase "less is more" during my interior design studies at LSU. The phrase was applied by architect Mies van der Rohe, speaking in the context of contemporary architecture. Anyone familiar with contemporary architecture will remember that Mies van der Rohe's work featured clean, straight lines free of clutter and complication. Contemporary and modern architecture always appealed to my neat-freak sensibilities, so it wasn't long before I began applying the "less is more" philosophy to other areas of my life (mainly finances).

The "less is more" idea seems counterintuitive, especially by American standards. America has always touted the values of "bigger is better" and "the more the merrier." Don't get me wrong: I hold absolutely no ill-will against those ideas. We have, as a country, achieved amazing feats because of them. However, we often fail to keep these values in perspective. The results are piles of possessions that get in our way instead of fulfilling their individual purposes. We, in turn, become so overwhelmed with the upkeep of our possessions that we are no longer fulfilling our purpose either. I experience this frustration every day in the micro-environment of my own kitchen cabinets. Michele and I have acquired somewhere around 20 hot/cold beverage cups. A few years ago, I gave in and spent some extra money on two Yeti containers, thinking that their quality would make all the other containers obsolete. I threw out all of the cheaper containers and was amazed at how well I de-cluttered. Unfortunately, my kitchen cabinets soon became re-cluttered with more beverage containers acquired from Christmas, birthdays, Father's and Mother's days, etc. The clutter was so bad that containers were literally flying out of the cabinets every time I opened the doors. It got to the point that I was unable to reach the kitchen equipment I actually needed or wanted to use regularly. The collection of stuff that was supposed to serve me was now dictating to me how to run my kitchen. Needless to say, I went through another round of de-clutter!

## Stuff Begets More Stuff

The world credits Mies van der Rohe with the phrase "less is more." I credit myself with the phrase "stuff begets more stuff." "Stuff begets more stuff" is the idea that most possessions require "accessory" possessions. These accessory possessions, which are necessary for servicing our mainstay possessions, soon add up to overpower our cabinets, closets, attics, and garages. A simple but effective example of this is any common lawn mower. A small push-mower that fits in the corner of any garage shouldn't cause much trouble, right? By itself, no. The problem is, you can't even start it if it's by itself. Unless you want to put it in your trunk and take it to the service station once a week, you'll need a gas can large enough to allow you to cut your yard a couple times. Don't forget some basic tools to work on the engine. While you're at it, you might as well pick up a box to store the tools. Need to sharpen the blade? No problem. Simply purchase a bench grinder and a workbench to bolt it to. Stuff begets more stuff. Stuff requires the presence of other stuff.

Boats present another great example of this effect. Boats take up a fairly large amount of space. If you are like most people whose garage can't swallow a boat and trailer, you'll need a cover or awning to store it. Before you head out for that first outing, make sure you pick up a life vest, throwable, fire extinguisher, and horn (if not equipped). In the state of Louisiana, you'll need a paddle. (Yes, I realize that paddling a ski boat is futile, but that's the law.) By the way, most of those items will mildew, rot, or rust if left in the boat year-round— they'll need to be stored inside, thus adding to the clutter.

Obviously, I'm not suggesting that you shouldn't own a boat. I'm definitely not suggesting you skip on a lawn mower, either. Your HOA will probably hunt me down if you do. What I do suggest is for you to consider the simplest form of either. Simpler items generally cost less. There are fewer moving parts to break down. They also require fewer tools and accessories. Less is more. Simple things beget less stuff.

The effect doesn't stop with large items. Some of our smallest possessions are the worst offenders. Try owning a smartphone... by itself. It can't be done! The first thing you need to do after purchasing a cellular phone is to present it with lavish accessories. You'll need a wall charger, a car charger, a USB adapter. Don't forget a strong phone case, lest your investment ends up with a shattered screen. Ear buds, charge pads, projectors, and laser keyboards round out the list. The list can grow as long as you are willing to allow. Multiply this times every phone, tablet, and laptop in your home, and you have the reason behind the mess of wires and plugs strewn about your countertops.

## Move Towards Minimalism

Is there anything particularly revolutionary about minimalism? I don't believe so. For my great-grandparents, minimalism was the normal state of life. The condition was so normal, in fact, they had no name for it. Compared to our modern standard of living, we wouldn't call it minimalism at all. Most would probably call it poverty. While I don't believe they were poor, I know for a fact that my great-grandparents had markedly fewer personal possessions. Their cars were very modest, and their homes were very small (in spite of the fact that their families were very large). My great-grandfather Felix only had a handful of prized possessions. A few well-used guns and knives, a watch, and a set of rosary beads were generally the only items my great-grandparents had to hold dear. My memories of and interactions with them tell me that they probably achieved a happiness far greater than most people can boast of today. The photos and stories I have of them seem to support that theory as well.

Like the kitchen cabinet, so full of useless stuff that we can't reach our best pots and pans, so are our lives. We spend so much time wading through and maintaining our wall of stuff that we can't reach the best parts of ourselves. We simply have no resources remaining to actually *do* the hobbies for which we accumulate the necessary equipment. We have no time left to participate in our communities. It's agonizing for me, as a hobbyist, wanting to try every hobby that's out there. I'm particularly fond of things in miniature. If I failed to discipline myself, I would fill the house with train layouts, slot car tracks, plastic models, and dioramas. Unchecked, I would spend thousands and become a hobbyist shut-in. I make a conscious decision every day to stick to one miniature hobby. It's far less expensive and it leaves me plenty of time for other pursuits. I've come to terms with the fact that I can't have it all. I can have a little bit and then share my remaining time and money with others.

## Learn to Pare Down

The first step on the road to simplicity is reducing clutter. My first rule of clutter is this: "If you haven't used it for over a year, you don't need it." Chances are, if you haven't used it for a year, you've actually forgotten that you have it in the first place. Which leads me to the second rule of reducing clutter: "If you forgot that you have it in the first place, you don't need it." These two rules alone can eliminate most of the common brick-a-brack found in the typical American household.

## Eliminate Redundant Items

Another quick method to reduce maximum clutter is to rid yourself of redundant items. Of all the areas of my household, the kitchen seems to be affected most by redundant stuff. Last time I de-cluttered, I was staggered to discover that Michele and I had four ice cream scoops! Who needs four ice cream scoops? You can only put one into the carton at any given time. Besides, we rarely have ice cream at home. When we do, it's no more than one small carton. Go through your kitchen. You probably have three sets of measuring cups. Keep the best quality set and toss the rest in the Goodwill box. We have a nice set of stainless measuring cups and spoons. How we ended up with two plastic dollar-store sets, I have no idea. I do, however, know exactly how Goodwill will end up with them. Don't even get me started on cheese boards. We managed to accrue five cheese boards in as many months. Here's an idea... host a reverse housewarming party. When you have friends over to celebrate your new home, provide the wine and cheese. Instruct your guests that gifts are strictly forbidden. Instead of receiving gifts, place all of your redundant household items into a barrel and insist that each of your guests take something home.

Electronics offer up their own special brand of redundancy. Smartphones have become so powerful that they can accomplish many tasks formerly dominated by computers. We also have the same features available in tablets and laptops. You won't be surprised to hear that I don't own all three. That's right, too much money spent on three items that all do basically the same things. I now have a smartphone, but I decided to pass on the tablet in favor of a laptop.

That brings me to my next lament on the topic of redundancy—navigation. Navigation systems add anywhere from $1,200 to $3,000 to the price of the average automobile. Often, the ridiculous prices of navigation units are justified by the addition of boundless extra features that most people will probably never use. Why am I picking on navigation units? Because everyone who owns a smartphone is already holding one in their hand! Smartphones should have rendered navigation units extinct years ago. Instead, our culture of mass consumption leaves us content to purchase two navigation systems: one in the car and one in our pocket. That's three navigation systems if you carry a tablet.

### Be Deliberate in the Purchasing of Goods

Wouldn't it be great if the simple life meant never having to buy any stuff at all? I wish that were the case. Alas, real life requires the consumption of goods and services. What really matters is how we approach our purchasing decisions. The number one question to ask is: "Do I really *need* this?" If you read my chapter on budget busters, you'll remember that our only true *needs* are food, water, shelter, and clothing. Let's be brutally honest, most of our "needs" aren't needs at all, they're just pretty big "wants."

I'm sure you've heard the phrase, "If it ain't broke, don't fix it!" I like to say, "If it ain't broke, don't replace it." How often do we replace items only because something newer or "bigger and better" becomes available? Televisions are a great example of this. Television technology changed very little from the time I was born (the mid-seventies) until about 2002. My family watched television on the same tube-style TV from 1975 until 1994. Back then, "big screen" TVs were prohibitively expensive and regular-sized TVs were very reliable. As a result, people kept televisions for many years. All that changed with the advent of the LCD and plasma screens.

When these large-format televisions hit stores in the early 2000s, they offered movie-theatre aspect ratios and much crisper resolution. In spite of their multi-thousand-dollar price tags, this first generation of flat-screen televisions flew off the shelves. Unlike their 70's-era predecessors, this new generation of televisions would be rendered obsolete before they were even plugged in for the first time. As a result, families who had purchased a $3,000 television in 2003 were often looking for the "upgraded" version by 2005. Nowadays, it's commonplace for people to replace their expensive televisions several times in the course of only a few years in order to keep up with the "latest and greatest" technology and the sharpest resolution.

If it ain't broke, don't replace it! When you keep a durable good through the entirety of its serviceable life, you inevitably replace it fewer times. Apply this idea to all of your durable goods and the savings will be monumental. I realize all this sounds an awful lot like common sense, but consider how many expensive items we replace that are still, in fact, useful. Televisions are reliable enough to last a decade or more. Is the miniscule increase in resolution worth thousands of dollars for a new unit? Consider keeping your television until it dies out. If that takes ten years, the increase in resolution over those ten years will absolutely be noticeable! Even better, you didn't spend thousands replacing something that actually worked. The same can be said for appliances as well. No matter how techie and cool the new refrigerators and washer/dryer sets are, you should never replace the ones you have until they are stone dead. If my great-grandparents saw me wheeling out a working refrigerator in favor of a new one, they would think I had *found* a suitcase full of money and *lost* my mind!

The over-replacement of goods doesn't stop there, either. Most people are replacing their phones each time the next generation hits stores. Many of these individuals are college students and young adults already saddled with massive student-loan debt. With smart-phone prices running from $500 to $1000, you can't convince me that all the old phones are even paid off before their owners are trading up. I imagine that they're rolling their negative equity into the next phone purchase. I've never seen the idea of obsolescence so power-fully demonstrated as in the case of smartphones. For a generation of young people who preach sustainability, throwing out a perfectly good $800 phone in favor of a $1,000 phone just seems very *un-sustainable.*

Really, what do you fear will happen if you fail to upgrade? In a world of iPhone Xs, I'm still sporting an iPhone 5s that was *given* to me. And guess what? Nothing bad happened as a result of my penchant for "obsolete" technology. I saved $1,000 on my phone and was able to use that money to replace something that had actually given up the ghost: my 11-year-old home computer. In retrospect, I used to wonder how so many people were running up $10,000+ credit card deficits. It wasn't on fine furnishings or the latest French fashions. As it turns out, many of these debts were due to the constant turnover of durable goods and electronics.

We've established that deliberate purchasing involves two ques-tions of need: "Do I really *need* this?" and "Is this item in *need* of replacement?" Once you have decided to move ahead with your purchase, it helps to evaluate the versatility of the items you are considering. Sometimes, a widget is a widget and its only purpose is to perform its stated task. Other times, you can save money and simplify your life by choosing a versatile widget. You might be surprised to discover that, sometimes, the simplest widget with the least bells and whistles turns out to be the most versatile. I find it especially easy to apply this idea in the kitchen, where storage space is already at a premium.

About twelve years ago, I picked up a copy of Alton Brown's *Gear for Your Kitchen.* At the time, I was enriching myself with knowledge on gourmet cooking and expecting his book to teach me all about the expensive pots, pans, and mixers I would "need" to further my culi-nary pursuits. Instead, I discovered a treatise on the hidden versatility of unsung everyday kitchen items that most of us already have. I learned that I didn't really *need* a double boiler for melting chocolate. A stainless bowl over a steaming pot of water would work just fine. A rice cooker? Forget about it! With a little research and some practice, I was cooking rice on the stovetop like a pro. Vegetable steamer? Replace the pan on the "double boiler" setup with a sieve and you'll have perfectly steamed broccoli in minutes. My family has actually gotten quite frustrated with my penchant for improvising so many so-called "invaluable" kitchen tools. My mom asks if I want a rice cooker for Christmas every year... every year I say no. Even now when I find myself believing that I "need" something, I scrounge around in search of an improvised solution rather than run out to make a purchase.

Deliberate purchasing is grounded in the reality of how an item will be used, not your fantasy. Deliberate purchasing demands that you do weeks, perhaps months, of research before making your purchase. A bike is a bike is a bike—or a kayak is a kayak is a kayak—just doesn't ring true. There are a myriad of very specific designs for each, and each design aims to fulfill a specific purpose. Finding the most versatile kayak for your needs can be like saddling up for a unicorn hunt. Such is true with most consumer items. Perform your research. Take advantage of any opportunity to test a product you are interested in. Make sure your selection is versatile enough to perform any task you may require of it. The result will be a more satisfying purchase that you are less likely to be posting on Craigslist next year for half of what you paid for it!

## Dude, Where's My Thirty-Hour Workweek?

The year I was born, the typical computer took up an entire warehouse and the personal computer was still several years away. It was very exciting to grow up at the dawn of the computer age. Elementary school computer classes often touted that technology would shorten the workweek and make our lives simpler. During college, the new availability of cellular phones and the internet brought the promise of a more connected tomorrow, where loneliness would be virtually eliminated. I think it's obvious that things didn't turn out quite that way. The cellphone that was supposed to be our lifeline in case of an emergency now threatens our safety every time we approach an intersection surrounded by texting motorists. Our devices have allowed us to accomplish more work than ever before, but that hardly matters when the average workplace just piles on more work. I've already established how our electronic devices are sapping our wealth. It's not a stretch to believe that all this additional time spent on social media and online gaming will lead to an even more unhealthy American population.

It probably sounds like I have a disdain for technology. That's partly true. More accurately, I am frustrated by those who are irresponsible in wielding it. I was once, in fact, a regular Facebook user. As part of our student government executive board, I voted to sign up our small college on this new, innovative social network. It was 2005 and Facebook was not yet available to the general public. At the time, Facebook was available only to students in participating colleges. With a student email address, you could take part in this "better" version of Myspace that promised seamless communication among the student body at your school. At first, Facebook was focused in its purpose and a joy to use. Have a group project in chemistry class with five students that you don't know? No need to pick up the phone or even email them individually. A quick announcement on Facebook ensured all of your group members knew when and where to meet. Oddly enough, Facebook was the first technology-based internet company I actually embraced. Alas, my infatuation was to be short-lived. By the time I graduated X-ray school, Facebook was open to the world. My inbox began to fill with "shower requests" and invitations to play everything from FarmVille to Mafia Wars. When I reached the point of spending 20 minutes a day clearing requests, it was time to move on.

It's hard enough to take on the minimalist philosophy when your neighbors are parading around in brand-new $50,000 SUVs. Seeing it all again on social media is plain disheartening. Unplug. If you don't see it, you can't envy it. While you're at it, cut off the cable (or streaming service), too. Once you parlay that time into tangible hobbies and exercise, your mind will feel less cluttered. You won't be continuously bombarded with the news of everyone's perfect life: their new cars, their dream vacations. I don't know if FarmVille is still a thing. If it is, try growing an actual garden instead. It's relaxing, rewarding, and will cut down your grocery bill. Share the fruits of your labor at work; it's a great way to make friends and foster relationships!

### Get in Touch with Your Inner Grandfather

If you are anything like me, your grandparents and/or great-grandparents were forced to survive during the Great Depression. My grandparents weren't exactly living hand-to-mouth, yet they had it pretty hard. My great-grandfather farmed, logged, trapped, and fished. He did all of that for the privilege of providing his family with a two-room house devoid of plumbing. Black Friday shopping sprees were non-existent; rather, Christmas saw each family member receive one small hand-made gift wrapped in brown paper and finished with bailing twine. An extra-exciting holiday season usually meant making some type of hard candy on Christmas Eve. And yet, I never heard my grandparents utter a syllable of regret regarding those holidays long-past. Instead, they always seemed to resent the hustle, stress, and disappointment that has come to represent the holiday season we know today. My grandparents endured a simplicity forged in necessity and steeped in survival. They were prime examples of the old American way. They forged ahead with hope and ingenuity. Want a lesson in the joy of simplicity? Put yourself in their shoes. What did they do for a living? What were their hobbies? How did your grandparents meet? How did they court?

Like many poor southerners, my great-grandfather on my father's side was a farmer. He continued to farm for a living until Eisenhower initiated the interstate system in the 50s. He was then able to go to work for the state highway department. He continued growing a large garden well into my childhood years. One of my last memories of him is grinding peppers that he had grown and dried. I decided last year that it was time for me to reconnect with my grandfather through the simplicity of living off the land. I prepared a small plot on my parent's property. My first crop was peanuts and peppers—the former being one of my great-grandfather's many depression-era cash crops and the latter his favorite hobby crop. I spent the summer of 2018 tilling, watering, pruning, and harvesting. I could picture my grandmother as a child winding through the bean poles as my great-grandfather toiled away at the year's harvest. The evening air would bring him the only available relief to the sweltering Louisiana heat. There would be no Netflix and chill, no emails to return, and no tweeting about the day's pickings. For his listening pleasure: crickets. His media: Mark Twain and other American classics.

I sliced away at the stems of each ripe pepper wielding one of the same knives he had used so many years ago. For me, it's one of many knives I've accumulated. For him, it was a prized possession, probably worth to him its weight in gold. As sweat ran constant off my brow, clothing sticking to my back, I was relieved to know that I would return from the garden to the air-conditioned comfort of my suburban paradise. A typical picking for my purposes lasted under an hour. My great-grandfather would have been out there from dawn 'til dusk. Long after his death in the fall of 1983, my great-grand-mother would tell me stories of their lives. She always cautioned me to be mindful of how much my generation has. She impressed upon me to be thankful for it. It has taken my entire life for those lessons to sink in. When I look back to their struggles, my own wants and "needs" seem pathetic. My home is much bigger, my cars are nicer... heck, I have *two* cars! I no longer care that my cars are used, or that my boat is small, or that my television is only 47". I want to turn back the clock, learn their skills, walk in their shoes, and know the happi-ness that permeated their rugged simplicity.

# 13

## CONTENTMENT

Somewhere, just inside middle age, it dawned on me. My dad was particularly blessed. I wish I'd had the wisdom to take notice sooner. Maybe I would've saved myself years of internal strife. To realize the level of God's blessings my father has enjoyed, I first had to put myself in his shoes. My father was blessed with a tight-knit, church-going family of hard workers. He was blessed with a God-given talent for math and science and, more importantly, the wisdom not to squander it. He was a success at work, and my life was made better for it. Dad inherited a beautiful piece of land to raise us on. My childhood was surrounded with loving family that assembled often for so many celebrations. Our family was largely free of drama, trauma, and family strife. Life wasn't always easy, fair, or perfect for our family; but I would choose it again given the choice. I have often pondered the issue of why God chose to bless my father so abundantly. I eventually concluded that my father is blessed simply because he is truly thankful and content with what God has granted him.

Dad never complained. I'm sure he could have found many things with which to be dissatisfied. He drove a small car that he kept for ten years. He had a small boat that he used for 25 years. Most people I know with older cars or boats talk constantly about upgrading. Dad could've gotten involved with expensive hobbies or leased hunting land. Instead, he was content to garden and hunt squirrel on the back of his property. My dad never showed off his income. As a matter of fact, you still can't pick him out of a crowd. He was content to live off far less than he earned, and he took time to help others along the way. For those reasons, I believe God chose to bless our family.

My dad understood the idea that all things are a blessing from God. Dad trusted in God's plan and never complained about his belongings or his station in life, and God blessed us all in return. Contentment leads to true happiness and thanksgiving, which results in greater blessings. Greater blessings bolster happiness and contentment. I never got the feeling that dad was waiting on the "next big thing" so he could be "set" or "have it made." My dad was always focused on where he was and what he was doing.

## Contentment

A simple life supported by discipline alone is hardly enough to achieve lasting peace, wealth, and happiness. If we are miserable with our current standing in life, we will not hold to the aforementioned values for long. A strong sense of contentment is necessary for us to be patient with our circumstances while we work toward our goals. Believing that humans are naturally ambitious creatures, I see no problem with looking into the future, dreaming of a better time and place. If we did not do so, we would not advance as a species. It is when we live totally in a daydream state that we lose our path. Overemphasis on our goals and expectations may lead to impatience and bitterness if not properly checked. My own dream of owning a boat, at times, has led me to become dissatisfied over my current pay or job position. Contentment is a powerful tool for calming the mind and finding happiness in the here and now. On the same token, dwelling on the successes and failures of the past can cause equal distraction.

Once again, I look to my father as a prime example of someone who has achieved great success because of his contentment with, and focus on, the present. My dad was able to find happiness in the simplicity of his life and possessions. He owned his things and they never owned him or our family. Because of this, he was able to quietly build wealth in a manner uncommon among modern American families.

Adhering to a cash-only lifestyle is not easy. You will see your friends, family, and neighbors driving the cars you wish you had. You'll see them wearing brand-name clothes while you're stitching the holes in your socks. They'll be sporting the latest handbags while you repair your own. Committing yourself to simplicity can go a long way in fueling your journey toward financial success, but it can only take you so far. Eventually, you have to make a mental shift. You have to change your internal dialogue from "I wish I had that" to "That would be nice to have, but I don't need it." You then progress to "I don't really want that anymore." Once you've reached the latter, you'll be surprised at how quickly you'll attain contentment. Contentment is the vehicle that carries us to a stark conclusion; we really don't need things after all. It is when we reach that point that we realize how blessed and privileged we really are.

A true sense of contentment with our current station in life helps us enjoy our blessings and keeps us focused on the here and now. Contentment allows our hearts to feel peace instead of the constant yearning for the many material things surrounding us. Living a cash-only lifestyle involves months (and sometimes years) of planning, saving, and strategizing. Many of those around you will be taking the quick and easy way by racking up debt. You'll never see their struggles, though. You will only see the expensive cars, nice clothing, and picture-perfect social media posts. A strong sense of contentment is paramount in dealing with the temptations you will inevitably feel. Contentment itself, like the cash-only lifestyle, does not come quickly and easily. It requires faith, focus, and mental discipline. Contentment, like any goal, is attainable and will make a positive difference in the way you feel about life. When you are happy with the things you have and happy with your place in life, your mind will be free to objectively plan your future without resenting the present.

I remember when I reached a place of true contentment. I remember literally running out of wants. My mind wasn't churning at 90 miles per hour trying to figure out how to attain that boat or when I would upgrade to a bigger vehicle. For the first time in my life, I didn't know what I was supposed to want. The feeling was disconcerting at first. Not having wants literally made me feel disassociated from myself, as if I had stepped out of my own body. I even mentioned to my therapist at the time that I didn't know what I was supposed to want next. She suggested I take some time to reflect before setting out on any new endeavors. Upon following her advice, I ascertained that I was happy with my place in life.

I'm not a psychologist or counselor, so I can't give researched tips on finding contentment. It's a complicated process. For some, including myself, it's as much a spiritual journey as it is a mental and practical exercise. What follows are some of my reflections on contentment and a few mental experiments that may move you toward answers to the great question of happiness.

## My Father: Master of Contentment

Before I found contentment, I was focused on tomorrow. I was waiting for that bigger boat or better job. I was holding my own happiness hostage. I wasn't focused on the many blessings I had right in front of me: a wonderful spouse, a fun job with a great income, a comfortable home, and two reliable, paid-for vehicles. Not to mention the fact that Michele and I have the most important blessing of all: good health. At first, focusing on happiness today did not come easy. I was afraid that I would neglect my plans for tomorrow. Happily, that hasn't turned out to be true. Finding contentment with my current situation has actually benefitted my future. I no longer force things. I don't make purchases simply because I am trying to "beat the clock" or "enjoy it while I'm young." I have surrendered my heart to God's plan. It will all happen at his will and in his time. For the time being, my job is to manage my life, marriage, and finances so that there will be a tomorrow to look forward to. Yes, that does require looking to the future; however, true contentment has given me the discipline not to *dwell* in the future. That, after all, was the balance my father found that allowed him to feel blessed and content in each moment.

### Enjoy What You Have

Sometimes we become so wrapped up in the promise of tomorrow that we neglect what we have right here and now. The accompanying internal dialogue might sound something like: "When I move up to a Denali, then I'll be set." "When I build that 2500 sq. ft. home, I'll be happy." I've experienced that same thought process from time to time, and boy does it kill your sense of contentment. My grandfather passed away fairly young, and that influenced my goal setting for many years. I wanted to "have it all" and "have it now" while I was young enough to enjoy it.

Many times, I resisted the temptations that came with that line of reasoning. Other times, I made ill-advised snap decisions. My car lease was a perfect example of this. The irony is that, had I taken my time (the one resource I thought I didn't have), I'd have been better off. My grandfather probably would have been proud of my zest for life. If he could speak to me now (sometimes I think he does), he would tell me to relax and enjoy each moment. That is certainly more precious than the things I dream of accumulating in the future. Nowadays, I tend to spend my time enjoying my things (my home, cars, and boat) in lieu of daydreaming about the ones I'll own tomorrow. After all, tomorrow's things are just fantasies anyway.

A mentor of mine once told an engaging story about contentment. I didn't understand it at the time. He refused to clue me into its meaning, saying only that, with time, I would understand. That story went something like this:

A young Native American warrior rode into a new village. He was tired from a long journey and was invited to sit with the tribal chief for refreshments. The old chief looked up slowly through the haze of campfire smoke and asked the young warrior, "Tell me about your tribe." The young man replied, "My tribe are a reckless people. They are selfish, thinking only of themselves. They never take the time to help others. I'm glad I left them and I hope to never return." The chief nodded in understanding and said, "You might want to continue on your journey young man. I think you will find our people are exactly the same."

The next evening, another young warrior rode into the same village. He, too, was tired from a long journey and was invited to sit with the tribal chief for refreshments. The old chief studied him carefully and asked, "Tell me about your tribe." The young man replied, "My tribe are a reckless people. They are selfish, thinking only of themselves. They never take the time to help others. I'm glad I left them and I hope to never return." The chief once again nodded in understanding and said, "You might want to continue on your journey young man. I think you will find our people are exactly the same."

Finally, a third warrior rode into the village the very next night. Again, he was tired from a long journey and was invited to sit with the tribal chief for refreshments. The old chief looked up slowly through the haze of campfire smoke and asked the young warrior, "Tell me about your tribe." The young man replied. "My tribe are a wonderful people. They are giving and kind, thinking only of others. They always take the time to help people in need. It hurt me deeply to have to leave them and I hope to one day return." The chief nodded in understanding and said, "You are welcome to stay with us young man. I think you will find our people are exactly the same.

The first few times I heard that story, I couldn't wrap my head around it. Did the old chief's tribe have a change of heart overnight? It took me a few years to realize that the tribe stayed the same. It was each young traveler's interpretations of their own people that were different. In other words, the young warriors who only saw the worst in their own people were likely to see the worst in their new surroundings as well. The third young warrior, who carried with him good thoughts of his own people, was likely to feel the same about the old chief's tribe. The old, wise chief saw this and considered it before extending invitations to stay with his people.

The message behind all of this? Happiness isn't derived from one's environment but from what one carries in their heart. People, good or bad, don't hold the keys to your contentment. The measurements of your home or the horsepower in your truck make no difference. The secret of contentment lies inside each one of us. Whether to be fully satisfied with our lives, miserable, or just "ok" is a decision that we make every minute of every day. Whatever our disposition is at the time is what will be carried into that new 4x4, house, or golf cart. That's why the "happiness" of things is so fleeting. Our purchases may provide us with a shot in the arm, but the medicine only lasts for so long. After the new car smell is gone and the glamorous house-warming is over, we are left only with what was inside of us in the first place. If emptiness and discontent fill that space, it won't be long until you're off searching for the next purchase.

### Focus on Today

Human beings are always wanting to rush to the next station in life. We express that desire through rites of passage. I was raised Catholic, and there were plenty of rites of passage to anticipate. At seven years of age, I completed my first reconciliation (confession), and I couldn't wait for my first communion. In the meantime, I forgot all about confession (been there, done that). I wanted to go to communion. After my first communion, I looked onward to earning my driver's license. I then looked to graduation, college, and graduation again. I remember that the joy of attaining each step was often fleeting and anti-climactic. None of those rites of passage led to sustained contentment. At the cusp of every achievement, I would feel great anticipation followed by an unsettling disappointment. I was focused on the next big event or the next rite of passage. I rarely stopped to take pleasure with my place and time in the moment.

The Star Wars universe recognized that very concept in *The Empire Strikes Back*. Yoda, frustrated with an impetuous Luke Skywalker, pokes his young apprentice with a stick and laments, "A long time this one I have watched as he looked away... Never his mind on where he was, what he was doing!"[1] Yoda was admonishing Luke for his lack of contentment with his station in life. Luke's impatience with his current situation left him frustrated and stripped of focus. Yoda understood that the adventure and excitement of tomorrow is a fantasy. It doesn't exist except in the mind. So, why live there at the expense of today?

The strangest part of this phenomenon of looking to the next station in life is that we always seem to want to go back to the last one. We couldn't wait to get out into the "real world." We thought we had it so bad with homework, curfews, and rules. As adults, we became bombarded with responsibilities we didn't realize our parents had. We then thought of how nice it would be to return to our adolescent lives that we once thought were so tough.

When I lived in my apartment many years ago, I longed for the day I would own a home. That home eventually took the form of a trailer (yes, I lived in a trailer) that I rented from my sister. During my time in the trailer, I had many nostalgic feelings for the old apartment while scraping together money to move up to a home. After a few years in my current home, I was surprised to start having those warm, fuzzy nostalgic feelings about my time in the trailer—not that I would want to go back there. As human beings, we always seem to be living in three places at once: the past, the present, and the future. There is certainly nothing wrong with memories of the past or hopes for the future, though it's important not to dwell on them at the cost of today. After all, yesterday and tomorrow only live in our imagination. Today is all we really have, so let's focus on it and make it the best day it can be!

## What Are You Trading?

In our rush to get to the "next big thing," we often fail to realize how much we are actually giving up. Getting out of that old beater and into a shiny new truck sounds great, but with that truck comes a lot of maintenance. With the average new truck costing $30,000-$35,000, you'll probably spend a lot more time cleaning and maintaining it than you do your current vehicle. After all, it wasn't that long ago that $30,000 was BMW money. I'd like to own a truck that nice one day (provided I can afford to have someone else maintain it). Before contentment, I was literally unable to enjoy a dirty car! When I think back to the countless beautiful weekends I spent washing, waxing, tire foaming, and Armor All-ing, I realize I could have spent that time actually enjoying my cars instead. Don't get me wrong, I still keep up my vehicles. However, I've been able to let go of my obsession with keeping them spotless. I was able to do that because I'm driving used, paid-for vehicles.

If I were to own, let's say, a brand-new 4Runner, I would cringe at the thought of taking it off road. With a base price of $35,000, it's not something I'm going to want to get dirty (in spite of its off-road prowess). My 2008 4Runner is an entirely different story. I bought it with plenty of imperfections. My happiness isn't derived from keeping it clean; on the contrary, I enjoy getting it dirty—very dirty. I can take it for a long weekend of camping and never worry about crashing through potholes, downed limbs, and wash-outs. Michele and I return from our outings with our truck wearing fresh scratches as badges of honor instead of marks of neglect. Old, paid-for vehicles look great filthy. As soon as I move into a nicer, more expensive vehicle, I give up that flexibility.

## Consumerism

Our consumer-centric society seems especially designed to erode our sense of contentment. Magazines, television, and social media bombard us with countless advertisements, images, and opinions that attempt to sway who we are and who we want to be. We are all compared to impossible standards of beauty and wealth. It's easy to lose sense of who we are in our attempt to fit the illusion. Magazines tell my wife that she's not attractive enough. Television tells me that my abs aren't defined enough. Commercials tell me that my car isn't cool, reliable, or safe enough. What can we do to tune out the noise?

I say avoid it all together. Limit social media. Ingest news and political commentary with a healthy sense of skepticism. Keep your mind open to both sides of an argument, but do your own research and fact-checking. Put away the magazines, or at least understand that their main purpose is usually to sell you stuff. When I was reading boat and car magazines, I was obsessed with boats and cars. I spent hours scheming about my next car or boat purchase. After I cancelled the subscriptions, I found I no longer thought of either. I quit wanting car and boat accessories, too. After all, if you don't know what's out there to want, you won't want it. Don't be so quick to follow trends. Trends blow in and out like a breeze. They leave you stuck with a closet full of junk that's out of fashion. I've seen this happen several times over the years with different trends; the "grunge" trend of the nineties is the one I remember most.

When I was in college in the mid-nineties, the grunge movement was well underway. Rock bands (though they were called "alternative" bands) eschewed the preceding era of rock decadence (the 80's "hair" bands). The calling card of the alternative rockers was the "grunge" look. It was the exact opposite of the over-the-top glamor of the hair bands. The grunge look involved tattered thrift-store clothing and greasy, unkempt hair. The idea was that the alternative bands were rebelling against materialism. Strongly associated with the grunge movement was a very popular shoe brand called "Dr. Martens," colloquially referred to as "Doc Martens."

A female co-ed of mine would drone on and on about materialism and the crimes of the capitalist mentality. During each diatribe, she would kick her feet up onto the courtyard table revealing her Doc Marten combat-style shoes. It struck me as ironic that someone so turned off by capitalism and materialism could spend $120 on a pair of brand-name shoes. It wasn't long before the fashions of the grunge movement became their own consumer-driven monsters. Doc Martens, baby doll dresses, goth makeup, and piercings were supposed to represent a rebellion against excess. Who knew rebellion against excess could be so expensive? The norms and trends aren't a rebellion if everyone else is doing it. You are the rebellion! Push back against consumerism for real by planning ahead, saving your money, and making careful, well-thought-out decisions with your money!

# 14

## DISCIPLINE

Self-discipline is the one value that allows us to put all other values and plans into action. So important is the role of discipline that it becomes, in essence, the gatekeeper of our plans; thwarting the temptations that aim to derail us from our goals. When we feel a desire to splurge, whether it be on a consumer item or an unhealthy snack, our discipline steps in to keep us on task. When our goal is to exercise regularly, discipline drives us to get up and jog or bike when it would feel so much better to remain in bed for another hour or so.

If my dad is a master of contentment, my great-grandmother was a beacon of discipline. When looking at our family's history, it's easy to see why. Even into her early eighties, my great-grandmother Bertine Loupe was up saying her Rosary every morning at 4am. The Rosary was followed by daily Novenas which preceded a breakfast of coffee, eggs, and toast. On Sundays, she was up extra early to bake homemade rolls. I saw that same level of discipline in my father. He rose early for work and returned home in the evening to exercise and tend garden. Neither watched much television and there was nary a vice between them. I have yet to achieve dad's or granny's level of self-discipline. In fact, I find discipline a difficult concept to define.

What exactly is discipline, anyway? Is it synonymous with self-control? Is discipline driven more by the urge to meet a goal or the fear of receiving a punishment? Is discipline a natural product of one's persona or an outcome of upbringing? I found these questions to be so challenging that I took a break from writing this chapter to research the subject. I am not a psychologist or sociologist. I won't attempt to propose an all-encompassing definition of discipline. For the purpose of this book, I will simply consider discipline to be the quantity of self-control necessary to accomplish a goal or avoid temptation. Discipline in finance, of course, may bleed over to other areas, such as health and fitness (which we discussed in Chapter 11), and we will touch on those ideas again. For now, let's look at some of the most important research that has been done concerning self-discipline.

## The Sweet Taste of Self-Discipline

Attempting to study the resistance to instant gratification in young children, psychologist Walter Mischel and his team developed a very simple test. Each participant was brought into a room one at a time and shown a marshmallow. The child was then presented with a choice. He or she could consume the marshmallow at any time, or wait for the researcher to leave for fifteen minutes and return. If the child was able to hold out for the entire fifteen minutes, he or she would receive a second marshmallow. The test was originally intended to study how the children who waited on the second marshmallow were able to do so. As it turns out, they were consistent in distracting themselves from the temptation of the one marshmallow that remained with them during the researcher's absence. Years later, when the participants began reaching college age, the experiment paid real dividends.

Apparently, Mischel's daughters were roughly the same age as the participants of the 1960's study. Mischel would occasionally hear news of those participants (now college age) and began to notice some interesting patterns. It seemed that the participants of the marshmallow study who did not wait for the extra marshmallow were more often ending up in personal and academic trouble. In an attempt to gather more information, Mischel sought out all the participants of the original study. He found that the children who delayed gratification in order to receive a second marshmallow were often times more successful than their counterparts who gobbled up the first marshmallow immediately. The delayed-gratification group also tended to exhibit better physical fitness and a lower propensity for drug use.[1]

The ideas I present in this book depend largely on the delayed-gratification aspect of self-discipline. A child waiting to eat a marshmallow with the hopes of receiving an additional marshmallow is very similar to an adult delaying gratification in exchange for a better car or more comfortable retirement later in life. The biggest difference in these scenarios is the time involved. The child in the marshmallow experiment needed only display his or her discipline for fifteen minutes. Your journey may span several years. How do you overcome impatience and temptation for a journey that will last years instead of minutes? For me, it starts with state of mind.

## State of Mind

I find discipline in personal finance to be very similar to that of diet and exercise. My father's heart attack at age 50 prompted me towards a low-fat, low-cholesterol diet at a very young age. In a way, I was very lucky. The fast-food burgers and fries that held so much appeal to me as a teenager began to look more like rat poison. I began reading the ingredients on the back of the snack-cake box and found the same sick feeling. Thinking of how sick my dad had become and the hell he went through, it wasn't all that difficult for me to change my lifestyle. Notice I said "lifestyle." Most people who spend time around me make the very natural assumption that I'm on a "diet." My co-workers see me heat up leftover turkey breast and green-beans or chicken and broccoli and ask, "How long have you been on that diet?" Of course, it's not a diet at all. Twenty years ago, I chose a healthy life-style. The fact that I chose a lifestyle instead of a diet is why I am successful. How do I measure that success? I weigh only a few pounds more than I did in high school. I don't suffer from many of the typical middle-age ailments, such as high blood pressure, diabetes, joint pain, etc. The numerical proof that my lifestyle is working fuels my resolve to stick with it.

My change in habits was not easy at first. Early on, you would have heard me say things like, "I can't have fried foods" or "I can't have fast food." I probably sounded like a typical person on a diet. As time progressed, the difference between dieting and adopting a life-style became more apparent. My state of mind made a major shift. My disposition made the conversion from "I can't have it" to "*I don't want it.*" Once I made that shift, the cornerstone was set. My lifestyle was determined.

For material items, I found the concept more difficult to apply. For many years, I watched my friends show off their hot rods and low riders. I spent Friday nights at the dragstrip wishing I had my own racecar to run the quarter mile. The remainder of my weekends were spent on the water ogling over everyone else's boats. I was very much in the "I can't have it" mentality. I remember vowing that, when I got my ducks in a row, I would own everything I wanted: A T-top Trans Am, a nice boat, a jet ski.

When I graduated X-ray school, I could have easily started signing up for payments on all those things. After all, I was single and paying next to nothing for rent. Interest rates were low at the time and the boating industry was in a slump, creating a buyer's market. I had promised myself all these things as a reward for finishing school, so what was the issue? My state of mind had shifted. Maturity perhaps? Or maybe I had worked so hard to succeed in school that I unlocked a level of discipline I didn't know I had.

For three years, I had attended class and clinic all day, commuted across town to work at the outlet mall folding endless piles of frazzled clothing. I would return home near midnight only to study several hours before catching a four-hour nap and returning to class. My weekends were tied up with work, study, and extra-curricular activities. I lived off of tuna, crackers, snack bars, and water. I knew the journey was going to be long and arduous, so I began to favor the journey over the destination. Over time, simplicity, contentment, and discipline became me. As that occurred, I suppose my goals became more altruistic. By the time I reached the end of X-ray school, I looked at my wonderful salary and thought, "I don't want to hand all of this to a bank. I want to keep as much of this as I can." I had moved from "I can't have it" to "I can afford this, but I don't really want it *that* bad." After I made that shift, financial discipline came much easier.

If you are in debt, you are probably feeling frustrated with seeing your hard-earned money slip away to the creditors with each passing pay period. You had probably grown up the way I did: dreaming about the day when you'd make great money and be able to buy all the cool things you wanted. Then life happened. The debt snuck up on you and, before you knew it, it seemed like an ocean of mud was poured between you and the financial freedom you had longed for. You picture yourself slogging through day after day, and you want to give up before you even take the first step. It's OK to feel frustrated! In fact, that's exactly what you'll need to succeed. Tap into your frustration and use it to motivate you. Stop paying "a guy" and discover your inner handyman (or woman). Get rid of that $700/month, six-year car loan and take pride in your cash vehicle. Smile when you start wearing holes through your socks but decide new ones can wait 'till Christmas. (Seriously, I never thought I would be happy to receive socks for Christmas... until I got so focused on paying off debt that I wouldn't even replace my holey underwear!) Over time, you will begin to identify with simplicity, contentment, and discipline. These three values will become you, and you will be able to move into the "I can have it, but I don't want it *that* bad" zone. Once you don't want it bad enough to go into debt, you can utilize your newfound discipline to budget, plan, and save your way to smart cash purchases.

## Running on Empty

When developing discipline, you should have a clear goal or purpose in mind. Discipline for its own sake can quickly begin to feel like torture. A perfect example of this would be my exercise routine. I lifted weights, albeit on and off. I could never muster the discipline to do weight training for more than about six months before becoming bored to tears. Jogging on a treadmill and running at the park bore slightly better results, but it often led to long stretches of avoidance due to burn-out or joint pain. I found discipline in exercise when I found biking. I never get bored with it. I look forward to my bike rides, and they have never resulted in joint problems or muscle pain. If I were to force myself to do weight training for discipline's sake, I would eventually fail and then chalk it up to poor discipline.

In the book *Willpower*, authors Roy Baumeister and John Tierney take a very interesting approach to the self-discipline debate. They postulate that individuals have a limited amount of willpower that can be used up by mental tasks, such as decision-making, temptation resistance, and self-control. Simply put, it is possible to tax your reserves of willpower to the point of failure.[2] I believe this line of reasoning because I have seen it at work in my own life. I have, at times, felt crushed under the weight of my own discipline. These challenges to my willpower often resulted in periods of sloth, over-spending, and overeating. After reading *Willpower* and reflecting on those times in my life, I realized that I was pushing my reserve of willpower past its limit. Authors Baumeister and Tierney suggest that, among other strategies, picking your battles and setting clear goals may help to alleviate this effect. Don't try to become perfectly disciplined at all things all the time and all at once. Instead, they suggest, pick a major goal and focus on just that project. Given enough time, the process becomes more automatic and demands less of our internal stores of willpower. A monthly budget, for example, is a perfect place to apply this idea. The first few monthly budgets you create may seem daunting. They will probably require lots of carefully researched decisions and often are not accurate to your household's actual needs. You will likely find it necessary to visit your budget app or spreadsheet on a daily basis for the first few months. Let your hobbies and other items lay for as long as it takes for the budget process to become automatic. When this happens, less of your self-discipline will be consumed by keeping your budget. It will simply fold into your daily routine.

## Built-in Discipline

In the pursuit of financial freedom, there are two main types of discipline we must observe. We must first develop the discipline to accomplish the tasks necessary to financial success: planning, budgeting, saving, tithing, communicating with our spouse, etc. Traditional methods of self-control—such as goal setting, time management, and rewards—help to spur us toward accomplishing those tasks. Those task-centered disciplines eventually become habit, and the discipline required to perform those tasks then becomes built-in. The second type of discipline necessary for financial success is temptation avoidance. Personally, I find temptation avoidance to be the easier of the two. Here are a few ideas to help avoid temptation while getting out of debt and saving for the future.

### Throw Out the Ads

As you are well aware, there is absolutely no lack of financial temptation out there. Everything can be financed, and large amounts of credit are available to just about anyone with a pulse. There are very few consumer items that can't be purchased in seconds via your computer, tablet, or smartphone. How can we stay focused when there is so much product out there that is so readily available? One way is to build up discipline by cutting out the temptation.

At one time, I received monthly subscriptions to car and boat magazines. By keeping the newest and best automobiles on my coffee table at all times, I was constantly rationalizing a new car—even as I was trying to get out of debt. I was making plans to wreck my newfound financial freedom before I'd even found it. And that's not to mention the many ads in those periodicals for all manner of boat and car-related products. I made a difficult choice to throw out the magazines and cancel the subscriptions. When I did, something amazing occurred: **I stopped wanting stuff!** My discipline to stay away from car lots and boat dealers is now built in to my system by virtue of the fact that I have removed one of the main temptations that drew me toward overspending. Saving a few bucks per month on the subscriptions is nice, too.

### Cut Up the Cards

Temptation exists anywhere there is a credit card. As long as there is plastic in your wallet (aside from a debit card), you risk wrecking your budget. It's a lot easier to head out for dinner after you've run out of money if you know you have that credit card to fall back on. Without a credit card, and without budgeted funds available for dining out, you'll be staying home until you have the money. Does that sound harsh? I think it sounds much harsher to pay for a dinner you ate a month ago. If you had cut up that credit card last month and payed it off for good, you wouldn't have had to pay that bill today. Voila! Money to dine out! As for online purchases, you'll think twice about buying it on debit because you are drawing from a finite resource. There is less chance that you will overspend because you know that your light bill has to come out of that account as well. These mental and emotional fail-safes don't exist with credit cards. I can't express this enough. **Cut up your cards!** After you've cut them up, be sure to call and cancel each one.

### Find a Distraction

Sometimes the best way to rid yourself of the static is to distract yourself from it. Find a positive hobby that you enjoy (preferably one that's inexpensive) and invest some of your time and energy into it. Hobbies don't have to wreck your budget to offer effective distraction from the many expensive and negative temptations that are out there. I've done many different hobbies over the years, and they have all played their own special role in my life.

From grade school into my twenties, I built plastic models. They were inexpensive, fun, and challenging. My enthusiasm for models kept me at home and out of trouble. I've dabbled in woodworking as well, having built several pieces of furniture for our home and a few chessboards just for fun. None of those projects cost much, and they gave me something to do during those times when money was tight and we were not able to go out to eat or take weekend trips. Most recently, I have taken up gardening. Seeds are cheap and dirt is free. Keeping up the peanut patch and the pepper rows provide great opportunities for outdoor exercise, and they yield a harvest of healthy food.

Whatever your distraction (models, crafts, gardening, painting), choose projects that will take a few sittings to complete. Pull them out on days when your budget is too tight to allow for other things. (If you are working hard to get out of debt, you'll definitely have those days.) A small project will distract you from the feeling that you're missing out and keep you focused on the future. The right hobbies can also help you develop patience and self-discipline (positively effecting your overall financial journey).

# 15

## FUTURE MILLIONAIRES OF AMERICA

Since I began writing this book in the summer of 2018, I've been on the lookout for a group of young people who I feel are putting into practice the financial ideas that I propose. During my research, I was fortunate enough to interview three outstanding individuals who are currently doing battle with societal norms in the quest to avoid debt. Each one is content with their current station in life, without forsaking their goals for the future. All three have embraced simplicity while thriving in an ever more complex world. They have mastered discipline in the face of monumental temptation and distraction.

I have assembled a group of stellar individuals I am convinced will be tomorrow's millionaires. I interviewed a young X-ray school graduate who is so determined to live a debt-free lifestyle that she has paid off over $12,000 in student-loan debt in one year. I also came to know a newlywed who is sharing her journey to debt freedom every day via social media. Speaking of social media, I had the pleasure of speaking with a 19-year-old college freshman who is building a landscape business and creating a leadership podcast while putting himself through business school debt-free! These individuals exemplify the ideas of personal responsibility, sound personal finance, and debt freedom.

Our first interviewee is Megan, who began working with me here at the emergency room nearly two years ago. During our many conversations, I began to discover that Megan is quite responsible with her money. I decided to interview her for this book hoping she could provide some insight on what it's like to pay off debt quickly and save for the future. Megan had very little help with college. In fact, she had saved up much of what she needed for college while still in high school. She has purchased two used vehicles with cash in order to save money and has amassed an impressive cash savings in only one year. What's even more impressive is how she is tackling her student-loan debt. Of her original $22,000 loan balance, she has already tackled $12,000 in only one year! I have no doubt that Megan has a bright financial future ahead of her! The following are Megan's financial statistics:

**Megan**
    Age:25
    Occupation:Radiologic Technologist
    Income:$45,000/year
    Student Debt:$10,000
    Rent:$580 w/utilities
    Credit Card Debt: 0
    Auto Debt:0

*Q. As a child, did you receive money in the form of allowance or gifts? Did you like to save it as opposed to spending it?*

A. I didn't receive allowance per se, but I would get money for birth-days and holidays. I really started saving at 16 so that I could buy a car. My brother had $10,000 saved long before he finished high school, and I had nearly $10,000 at high school graduation.

*Q. Were your parents big savers?*

A. My parents acted like they had no money. Then they would come up with cash for renovations, cars, etc. The key is to live like you're poor so that you actually have money.

*Q. How do you handle preparing for emergencies?*

A. I've always kept a cushion. At first, my cushion was $1,000. I never let my account go below that in case of emergencies. After a few years, I considered $6,000 to be my cushion. Now, my cushion is $10,000.

*Q. At what point did you realize that you treated money differently than your peers?*

A. High school. I worked part time and I never had to ask my parents for money. When I was out with friends and refused to buy things for them, they called me "stingy." I graduated with $10,000. One of my friends once saw one of my ATM receipts. She freaked out! Before that, I thought everyone was saving like me.

*Q. Did your viewpoint on money ever create problems in your relationships?*

. . .

A. I'm always the breadwinner in every relationship. My boyfriends have always lived paycheck to paycheck. I don't think anyone should be dependent on anyone else in a relationship. The only person you can rely on is yourself.

Q. *You paid cash for a used car off Craigslist. Do you have any regrets about that decision?*

A. No. Not one.

Q. *Do you feel your car is safe and reliable? Has anything bad happened as a result of your decision to drive a used car?*

A. Both used cars I've owned have been safe and reliable. Neither one has been problematic.

Q. *What about your peers? Do you know of anyone else driving a used car and paying off debt?*

A. I don't know anyone else that has bought their own car for cash.

Q. *You took out some loans to pay for X-ray school? How much did you originally owe?*

. . .

A. $22,000.

Q. *Have you made progress on paying that off?*

A. I've paid off $12,000 in the past year.

Q. *So you've paid off $12,000 in about one year. What kinds of sacrifices does that require?*

A. I lived with my parents for a while. I've since moved out, but only after saving $10,000 for emergencies.

Q. *Your student loans are your biggest (and only) debt. What is your plan after you pay off your student loans?*

A. The money I am currently paying towards loans I will probably use to save for another car and a down payment on a home.

Q. *Any retirement goals?*

A. I am currently saving 6%. I am going up one percent each year. After I pay off my student loan, I will bump it up more than that.

Some of Megan's sentiments concerning her peers sound very similar to the ones I had in high school and college. I can especially relate to being called "stingy" or "tight." It's obvious that Megan is thinking about the road ahead and wanting to free up the full power of her earnings by getting rid of her debt as quickly as possible. I have a feeling she will be very successful, and I would be very surprised if she ever decides to take out a loan for anything other than a home. I was, however, surprised by her response to a question about retirement. I asked Megan if she was aiming for millionaire status. In spite of her very good choices and stellar earning potential, she had never considered the goal attainable. Using a simple online retirement calculator, I plugged in Megan's salary along with a 15% investment into her employee-sponsored Roth 403(b). I estimated a very conservative 6% growth, and Megan was floored by the results. Even if Megan never receives a raise, an annual contribution of 15% of her $45,000 salary will result in a retirement nest egg of over 1 million dollars! That begs the question: If someone like Megan with such incredible foresight and money skills considered millionaire status unreachable, how many others are out there not realizing their financial potential?

Our next interviewee is Jenn Nguyen. Jenn and her husband are newlyweds who are facing a debt of $129,000 (mostly attributable to student loans). Jenn has been very generous in sharing her journey to debt freedom on social media sites such as Instagram. Jenn is a teacher and has a special message for her peers. She would like other teachers to know that, in spite of their income, they can attain debt freedom and achieve millionaire status!

## Jenn

    Age:29
    Occupation:Teacher
    Income:$140K (including spouse)
    Student Debt:$109K
    Mortgage:$218K
    Credit Card Debt: $800
    Auto Debt:$0

. . .

Q: *In your opinion, what is the biggest challenge facing families who are trying to get out of debt? What are the biggest budget busters?*

A: Getting my spouse on the same page was my biggest challenge. We just got married and combined our finances, so it's hard for him to see a smaller amount of money in his personal account. Our biggest budget buster is eating out. Work keeps us busy and sometimes my husband doesn't come home until 7:30 pm on the weekdays, so when the weekend hits, we're just exhausted, so we go out to eat.

Q: *When did you first begin to learn about personal finance?*

A: My parents have always been really good with handling money. They came to this country with nothing and built an amazing life together, making sure my siblings and I had what we needed (there's five of us). Ever since I can remember, on Fridays, when my dad got paid, he would write down a budget, making sure he saved some of his check. When I got my first job at 15 (going to work with my dad, getting paid $5 an hour), my parents taught me to save some of my money. It helped me develop good saving habits.

Q: *When did you decide to pursue a debt-free lifestyle?*

A: My husband and I have always talked about starting this lifestyle, but life got in the way (saving for a ring, house, furniture, wedding, etc.). Now that we're married, this was naturally the next step for us:

following in both our parents' footsteps by living a simple, debt-free life.

Q: *Did you encounter any naysayers along your journey? Anyone attempting to dissuade you from your plans?*

A: Luckily, everyone in our lives is very positive and understands what we are going for. Some of my husband's old classmates don't understand, however. They are waiting to get their loans forgiven in 25 years because they think that's the best thing to do. One of my husband's cousins was surprised when I told him that we were finally able to save just for the sake of saving. That was when I realized not everyone has a savings, but that's a different story.

Q. *What role has contentment, discipline, and simplicity played in your journey towards financial freedom?*

A: It plays a huge role. For example, I just got paid today and literally every penny of my paycheck is gone. It went to the mortgage, our student loans, a credit card, and a little to savings (always pay yourself). I am living on what little I had from my last paycheck for the next two weeks.

Q. *You share your journey toward debt freedom on Instagram. How has social media benefited you during your journey?*

.  .  .

A: It helps me stay focused and keeps me accountable. I love knowing that there is a community of people out there doing the same thing I am and cheering me on.

Q: *You and your husband started in January 2018 paying off over $129,000 in debt. In only six months, you've managed to reduce that total by nearly $25,000. What is your secret?*

A: We throw anything we can on our debt when we can. We eat at home, give ourselves an allowance, and basically spend all our free time at home doing something low cost for fun, like riding our bikes.

Q: *You are on track to pay off your remaining debt in six years. How do you plan to celebrate?*

A: I don't even know how we'll celebrate! Today, I am just focused on little steps forward.

Q: *What words of encouragement would you like to offer to other teachers who wish to become debt-free?*

A: It's not what you make, it's how you spend it. Be wise with your paychecks and know there's always someone out there who has it worse than you.

You can share in Jenn's journey by following her on Instagram *@coffeeandjenn.*

. . .

Representing a new generation of debt-free college students is Kyle Hammers. Kyle is a 19-year-old college freshman who is determined to earn his degree without using student loans. Kyle is also the voice of the *Lead by Example Podcast*, where he interviews leaders in business, sports, and personal finance.

**Kyle**
  Age:19
  Occupation:Student/Landscaper
  Income:$40-$60/hr.
  Student Debt:$0
  Mortgage:$0
  Credit Card Debt: $0
  Auto Debt:$0

*Q: How did you become interested in personal finance?*

A: I picked up a copy of *The Total Money Makeover* one day without any rhyme or reason. It was just sitting on our coffee table at home and I was bored. I remember thinking to myself: "This Dave Ramsey guy seems kind of crazy, but what could it hurt to read it?"

*Q: Did you learn sound finance skills from your parents, or was your interest stoked by other means?*

A: My parents have been great examples for me, and I've learned a lot about personal finance from their journeys. They have had their fair share of financial binds before, so being able to see them at those low points and how they fought to recover has been huge for me. Outside of that, I've done a lot of self-teaching through reading books.

Q: *How do your peers react to your ideas about personal finance?*

A: When I started catching on to what some of the financial gurus were saying about money, it lit me on fire. I was still in high school at the time, and I was pretty vocal about my beliefs when it came to personal finance. A lot of people began to look at me the same way I looked at Dave Ramsey before I read his book: crazy.

Q: *Are many of your peers already in debt?*

A: I am a freshman in college, so not too many of them have had the opportunity to get into debt, aside from student loans. I know there are quite a few who went away to college and are attending private institutions, and they are definitely in student-loan debt. That is all I am aware of though!

Q: *Do you believe that it is possible to earn a college degree without taking on student debt?*

A: Absolutely. If you don't agree, then you should read the book *Debt-Free Degree* by my friend Anthony O'Neal. He has devoted his life to showing how there are so many ways to pay for higher education. There are just so many opportunities out there: scholarships, grants, financial aid, and work-study programs, just to name a few.

. . .

*Q: I understand that you are running your own lawn care business. Tell me a little about that.*

A: I started a mowing business as a way to make money, especially through school. It allows me to make anywhere from $40-$60/hr. versus a minimum-wage job under $10/hr. This allows me to work less and still make more; giving me tons of time to focus on my studies and start a podcast. My podcast will be a gateway into the online business world that I am looking to grow in the future!

*Q: What is the message that you would like to pass on to your peers in Generation Z?*

A: Get educated. You can make personal finance as complicated or as simple as you want it to be. I would start with the basics like Dave Ramsey's baby steps and go from there! Simple strategies like living on less than you make can really pay off in the long run. The second piece of advice I would give is to start investing today! Compound interest is real and your time to take advantage of it is now!

*Q: What role does simplicity, discipline, and contentment play in your life? In your financial strategy?*

A: They are all huge, and all three support each other. When it comes to financial strategy, I believe in not overcomplicating it. Personally, Dave Ramsey has been my biggest inspiration because he has not only built a successful personal-finance portfolio, but a business that is now valued at 250 million dollars. He has done all of that by doing "God's and grandma's way of doing money." Keep it simple, stupid.

Q: *You have recently started your own podcast centered around leadership. Tell me about the purpose and message behind the Lead by Example Podcast.*

A: I believe there are so many traits a leader can and should possess, but it all comes down to one thing: putting them into practice. That is where the Lead by Example brand comes into play. I want to help people become leaders, especially in areas of business. My goal is to land conversations with people who are leaders in their respective areas and bring those conversations to my audience while networking along the way. I'm super passionate about this, and I would love for anyone to listen to the podcast and reach out to me.

Q: *What are your plans after college?*

A: To be completely honest, I don't know. My plan right now is to pursue a career as a financial advisor, then a CFP. However, leadership is my true passion, and that's a broad category. If God calls me to something else, I am totally open to that. I was put here on this earth to do one thing and that is to glorify him in whatever I do.

# THE CASH DIET LEGACY

April, 2020. Like the alien invaders from H.G. Wells' *War of the Worlds*, whose superior technology could not protect them from a simple virus, the American financial system crumbles at the feet of Covid-19. How could a simple bundle of proteins bring an entire economic system to a grinding halt? The answer is simple: debt. Every person in the corporation that is America—from the man that mops the basement floor to the CEO in the penthouse—is in debt to someone else. A shutdown in the flow of cash at any point in the chain disrupts the entire system. When everyone in the system owes everyone else and has no cash stored for emergencies, no person in the system can pay the person above or assist the person below. Such was the legacy of Covid-19.

As I type this conclusion, my wife is on furlough from her employer, and there has been serious discussions of hourly cuts at my own workplace. For us, the legacy of Covid-19 will not be one of worry and strife. We have designed our lifestyle so that we can function on only one income. Our emergency fund can sustain us for ten months if neither one of us are able to work. Ours will be the Cash Diet legacy, where we are able to continue paying our mortgage while helping those around us. I often tell friends that Murphy's Law works both ways. Since we have an emergency fund, it's likely that Covid-19 will pass long before we have to use it. If we didn't have the means to weather this storm, I'm sure Murphy would be standing in our front yard right now. What will be your legacy?

# ABOUT THE AUTHOR

 X-ray tech Christopher Savoy is the "Cash Budget Cajun." After a series of financial disasters, he returned to the lessons of his childhood about thrift, self-reliance, and the simple life. Today, he preaches old wisdom to new generations. A lifelong Louisiana Cajun, Christopher is an Eagle Scout, gardener, and fisherman who believes any problem can be solved with a hot cup of coffee and a greasy ballcap. He holds a master's degree in radiologic science and lives the good life in Baton Rouge with his wife and two dogs.

# ACKNOWLEDGMENTS

A special thanks to my entire family for the best childhood a kid could ever ask for. My sister and I wanted for nothing and were embraced by love, encouragement, and patience. To my Aunt Peggy and Uncle Wayne, and my best friend's parents Paul and Valeda, who set wonderful examples of stable, loving family life. To my lovely wife, Michele, who puts up with my constant obsession with the budget as well as my many hobbies and interests. Her love, acceptance, and encouragement has allowed me to grow well beyond the limitations that I would have settled for had she not come into my life.

Thanks also goes out to my colleagues, who were a constant source of encouragement throughout the writing of this book. To Leona Babin, Brenda Sterling, and Patrice Pujole: the best three English teachers in Louisiana's public schools. They each recognized my talents, pushed me hard, and never allowed me to turn in work they felt was not up to my highest capability. For my cousin Claire, who's dream of becoming a writer was cut short by tragedy. For Piper. You had the heart of a lion and we will never forget you.

# BIBLIOGRAPHY

"21% of Divorcees Cite Money as the Cause of Their Divorce, Magnify Money Survey Shows." Magnify Money. February 13, 2017. Accessed January 5, 2019. https://www.magnifymoney.com/blog/featured/money-causes-21-percent-divorces925885150/.

"50-Year Loan Debuts in California." Bankrate.com. April 27, 2006. Accessed February 24, 2019. https://www.bankrate.com/finance/mortgages/50-year-mortgage-debuts-in-california-1.aspx.

Allison, Tom. "Financial Health of Young America: Update – For the First Time, Young Adults with Student Debt Have Negative Net Wealth." Young Invincibles. April 2018. Accessed February 15, 2019. http://younginvincibles.org/wp-content/uploads/2018/04/Financial-Health-of-Young-America-update.pdf.

"Average Annual Boating Days by Boat Type in the U.S. 2013." Statistica.com. 2013. Accessed April 5, 2019. https://www.statista.com/statistics/240522/recreational-boating--average-annual-boating-days-in-the-us/.

"Average Phlebotomist Salaries in the United States." Indeed.com. Last modified May 1, 2020. https://www.indeed.com/salaries/phlebotomist-Salaries.

Baumeister, Roy F. and John Tierney. *Willpower: Rediscovering the Greatest Human Strength*. New York: Penguin, 2012.

Casey, B. J., et al. "Behavioral and Neural Correlates of Delay of Gratification 40 Years Later." *Proceedings of the National Academy of Sciences* 108, no. 36 (September 6, 2011): 14998–15003. https://doi.org/10.1073/pnas.1108561108.

"CFPB Report Finds Sharp Increase in Riskier Longer-Term Auto Loans." Consumer Finance Protection Bureau. November 1, 2017. Accessed January 4, 2019. https://www.consumerfinance.gov/about-us/newsroom/cfpb-report-finds-sharp-increase-riskier-longer-term-auto-loans/.

Desilver, Drew. "5 Facts about Today's College Graduates." Pew Research Center. May 30, 2014. Accessed January 3, 2019. https://www.pewresearch.org/fact-tank/2014/05/30/5-facts-about-todays-college-graduates/.

Federal Reserve Bank of New York, Research and Statistics Group. "Quarterly Report on Household Debt and Credit." Center for Microeconomic Data. February 2018. https://www.newyorkfed.org/medialibrary/interactives/householdcredit/data/pdf/HHDC_2017Q4.pdf

Hammers, Kyle. Interview via electronic correspondence. October 2019.

"How America Saves for College 2018." Sallie Mae. 2018. Accessed February 9, 2019. https://salliemae.com/about/leading-research/how-america-pays-for-college/.

"How Much Does a Phlebotomist Make in the United States?" Indeed.com. Last modified May 1, 2020. https://www.indeed.com/career/phlebotomist/salaries.

Irvin Kershner, dir., *The Empire Strikes Back*. 1980. United States: 20th Century Fox. Motion picture.

Keown, Arthur J. *Personal Finance: Turning Money into Wealth*, 3rd ed. New York: Pearson, 2003.

Kessler, Aaron. "Auto Leasing Gains Popularity Among American Consumers." *The New York Times*. January 8, 2015. Accessed January 4, 2019. https://www.nytimes.com/2015/01/09/business/auto-leasing-gains-popularity-among-american-consumers.html.

"Lease Market Report: January 2017." Edmunds.com. January 2017. Accessed February 15, 2019, https://dealers.edmunds.com/static/assets/articles/lease-report-jan-2017.pdf.

McKim, Jenifer. "More Seniors Are Taking Loans Out Against Their Homes—and It's Costing Them." *The Washington Post*. August 25, 2017. Accessed February 13, 2019. https://www.washingtonpost.com/business/economy/more-seniors-are-taking-loans-against-their-homes--and-its-costing-them/2017/08/25/5f154072-883a-11e7-961d-2f373b3977ee_story.html.

Megan. Personal interview. April 5, 2019.

Mischel, Walter, E.B. Ebbesen, and A. Raskoff Zeiss. "Cognitive and Attentional Mechanisms in Delay of Gratification." *Journal of Personality and Social Psychology* 21, no. 2 (1972): 204–218. https://doi.org/10.1037/h0032198.

Mischel, Walter, Yuichi Shoda, and Monica L. Rodriguez. "Delay of Gratification in Children." *Science* 244, no 4907 (May 26, 1989): 933–938. https://doi.org/10.1126/science.2658056.

Nguyen, Jenn. Interview via electronic correspondence. September 2019.

Oakley, Diane, Jennifer Erin Brown, and Joelle Saad-Lessler. "Retirement in America: Out of Reach for Working Americans?" National Institute on Retirement Security. September 2018. Accessed January 4, 2019. https://www.nirsonline.org/reports/retirement-in-america-out-of-reach-for-most-americans/.

"Post-Graduate Debt & Spending Survey." Accounting Principles. November 2, 2018. Accessed January 3, 2019. https://www.accountingprincipals.com/employers/employer-resources/post-graduation-debt-and-spending-survey/.

Shoda, Yuichi, Walter Mischel, and Philip K. Peake. "Predicting Adolescent Cognitive and Self-Regulatory Competencies from Preschool Delay of Gratification: Identifying Diagnostic Conditions." *Developmental Psychology* 26, no. 6 (1990): 978–986. https://doi.org/10.1037/0012-1649.26.6.978.

Zabritski, Melinda. "State of the Automotive Finance Market," Experian, January 15, 2020. Accessed My 28, 2020. http://www.experian.com/automotive/automotive-credit-webinar.

# NOTES

## 2. Reduce Your College Debt

1. "Post-Graduate Debt & Spending Survey," Accounting Principles, November 2, 2018, accessed January 3, 2019, https://www.accountingprincipals.com/employers/employer-resources/post-graduation-debt-and-spending-survey/.

## 3. The Career Stairstep

1. "How Much Does a Phlebotomist Make in the United States?" Indeed.com, last modified May 1, 2020, https://www.indeed.com/career/phlebotomist/salaries.
2. "Average Phlebotomist Salaries in the United States," Indeed.com, last modified May 1, 2020, https://www.indeed.com/salaries/phlebotomist-Salaries.

## 5. Retirement Savings

1. Diane Oakley, Jennifer Erin Brown, and Joelle Saad-Lessler, "Retirement in America: Out of Reach for Working Americans?" National Institute on Retirement Security, September 2018, accessed January 4, 2019, https://www.nirsonline.org/reports/retirement-in-america-out-of-reach-for-most-americans/.
2. Melinda Zabritski, "State of the Automotive Finance Market," Experian, January 15, 2020. Accessed My 28, 2020. https://www.experian.com/automotive/automotive-credit-webinar.

## 6. 'Till Debt Do Us Part

1. "21% of Divorcees Cite Money as the Cause of Their Divorce, Magnify Money Survey Shows," Magnify Money, February 13, 2017, accessed January 5, 2019, https://www.magnifymoney.com/blog/featured/money-causes-21-percent-divorces925885150/.

## 7. The Dealer Always Wins

1. "Lease Market Report: January 2017," Edmunds.com, January 2017, accessed February 15, 2019, https://dealers.edmunds.com/static/assets/articles/lease-report-jan-2017.pdf.
2. "CFPB Report Finds Sharp Increase in Riskier Longer-Term Auto Loans," Consumer Finance Protection Bureau, November 1, 2017, accessed January 4, 2019, https://www.consumerfinance.gov/about-us/newsroom/cfpb-report-finds-sharp-increase-riskier-longer-term-auto-loans/.


## 8. Your First Home

1. "50-Year Loan Debuts in California," Bankrate.com, April 27, 2006, accessed February 24, 2019, https://www.bankrate.com/finance/mortgages/50-year-mortgage-debuts-in-california-1.aspx.
2. Jenifer McKim, "More Seniors Are Taking Loans Out Against Their Homes—and It's Costing Them," *The Washington Post*, August 25, 2017, accessed February 13, 2019, https://www.washingtonpost.com/business/economy/more-seniors-are-taking-loans-against-their-homes--and-its-costing-them/2017/08/25/5f154072-883a-11e7-961d-2f373b3977ee_story.html.


## 9. Toys, Travel, and Hobbies

1. Diane Oakley, Jennifer Erin Brown, and Joelle Saad-Lessler, "Retirement in America: Out of Reach for Working Americans?" National Institute on Retirement Security, September 2018, accessed January 4, 2019, https://www.nirsonline.org/reports/retirement-in-america-out-of-reach-for-most-americans/.
2. "How America Saves for College 2018," Sallie Mae, 2018, accessed February 9, 2019, https://salliemae.com/about/leading-research/how-america-pays-for-college/.
3. "Average Annual Boating Days by Boat Type in the U.S. 2013," Statistica.com, 2013, accessed April 5, 2019, https://www.statista.com/statistics/240522/recreational-boating--average-annual-boating-days-in-the-us/.


## 13. Contentment

1. Irvin Kershner, dir., *The Empire Strikes Back* (1980; United States: 20th Century Fox), motion picture.

## 14. Discipline

1. Walter Mischel, E.B. Ebbesen, and A. Raskoff Zeiss, "Cognitive and Attentional Mechanisms in Delay of Gratification," *Journal of Personality and Social Psychology* 21, no. 2 (1972): 204–218. https://doi.org/10.1037/h0032198; Walter Mischel, Yuichi Shoda, and Monica L. Rodriguez. "Delay of Gratification in Children," *Science* 244, no 4907 (May 26, 1989): 933–938. https://doi.org/10.1126/science.2658056; Yuichi Shoda, Walter Mischel, and Philip K. Peake, "Predicting Adolescent Cognitive and Self-Regulatory Competencies from Preschool Delay of Gratification: Identifying Diagnostic Conditions," *Developmental Psychology* 26, no. 6 (1990): 978–986. https://doi.org/10.1037/0012-1649.26.6.978.

2. Roy F. Baumeister and John Tierney, *Willpower: Rediscovering the Greatest Human Strength* (New York: Penguin, 2012), 88-93.

CPSIA information can be obtained
at www.ICGtesting.com
Printed in the USA
LVHW030209290121
677803LV00038B/803/J